WHO DO YOU SAY I AM ?

CHRIS THOMAS

For my adopted aunty,
Maureen Mills,
whose loyalty and faithfulness
to me and my family for over
60 years has both inspired me
and at times comforted me.

WHO DO YOU SAY I AM ?

First published in 2019 by
New Life Publishing, Luton,
Bedfordshire LU4 9HG

© Chris Thomas

British Library Cataloguing in Publication Data
A catalogue record for this book is available
from the British Library

ISBN   978 1 912237 19 7

Unless otherwise stated Bible references are
from the New Jerusalem Bible, Darton, Longman
and Todd, UK (1985) and are used with permission.

Typesetting by New Life Publishing,
Luton, UK   www.goodnewsbooks.co.uk
Printed and bound in Great Britain

CONTENTS

Introduction 1

1. Who am I and Who are You? 5

2. Jesus, the Lamb of God 21

3. Searching for God 37

4. Gentle Jesus Meek and Mild - *Really*? 51

5. The Jesus Experience 65

6. Suffering for the Sake of the World 79

7. The Inclusivity of God 93

8. More Than We Deserve 106

9. Called to Serve 121

10. Let My People Go 135

11. Freedom and Mercy Go Hand in Hand 149

12. Freed to Live 163

Conclusion 177

INTRODUCTION

Ever since my encounter with Jesus, which you can read about in other books I have written, I have been fascinated with the person of Jesus Christ. I am intrigued by this man with his immense compassion and love and depth of humanity. It is something that has inspired people down the centuries to discover what it means to be fully alive and fully human. Equally I am in awe at the truth we, as Church, have arrived at after centuries of reflection, that he is not only a human being but also completely and fully divine. That is something I believe in my guts and yet find it difficult to put any sort of language on it. I live with a constant tension asking the question, 'Who are you?' I never discover enough to answer it. I suppose that means there is always more in God. The mystery is too impenetrable and yet it pulls and draws us more deeply into something which is extraordinarily life-giving. We can enter into the mystery and discover life through that mystery as countless generations have witnessed.

I suppose because of all that, the question that Jesus faced his disciples with, 'Who do you say I am?' has always captured my attention and I hope yours too. How are we going to answer it? It is not enough to simply come to a dogmatic belief that Jesus is God because Sr Mary told us that in 1937. Nor is it enough to simply trust when we were told that Jesus was a human being.

It is not enough, for me, to think that because we believe in the truth we were taught as children, we have entered into the relationship that God wants us to have with God. It is a deeper call than that and it involves asking who is Jesus for me? Not just who is Jesus, but who is Jesus for me? Who is Jesus logically? Does he make sense? Who is Jesus really? Who is he in real life, for me? Do I have a living personal relationship with him? Is he the centre of life for me? You see, we are being drawn into something much deeper and much more radical which, if we take it seriously, will affect the very core of our being.

Each of the evangelists give us a different insight into the person of Christ. Four different faces leading us more deeply into the mystery of Christ. Matthew, Mark, Luke, and John are not interested in giving us biographies of Jesus. They are interested in inviting us into a relationship. It seems that most of us need to have a strict biography of Jesus. We want first-hand accounts that tell us what he really did and how he really did it and when it happened. I think in many cases we are asking the wrong questions and we force the evangelists to meet our needs. The Scriptures invite us to explore meaning which for the ancient peoples was far more important than our one dimensional sense of truth and the interminable question, 'did it happen?'

As I said above, the Gospels are not concerned with giving us a biography of Jesus. They are not concerned with giving us a series of prescriptions and doctrines and dogmas. They are probably not overly concerned with teaching us about eternal truths. They are interested, as individuals and as communities, in giving a description of a person who has saved them and freed them and loved them.

So, I am not sure that this book will be a tidy exploration of the theological understanding of Christ. However, what I would like to try and do in this book is to explore, albeit at a superficial level, the image of Christ that each evangelist gives us and what that means to me. I will probably take wild leaps into the mystery without always understanding what I am saying but I hope that it adds more to my encounter, and yours, with this Christ who is at the centre of my life and who is always calling me more deeply into him and therefore into life.

ONE

WHO AM I
AND WHO ARE YOU?

I was at a young people's camp in Dublin in the mid 1970's. I had gone with all the enthusiasm of youth and with some friends to explore the Gospel. I have to say it was a formative time in my life as I grew in faith and as my desire for God overwhelmed me more and more. The weather was beautiful the whole time we were there. One particularly hot summers day, along with my friend Jane and her future husband Tony, we went outside to pray.

I am not sure that I can ever explain what happened, but we began to sing the hymn 'Father I believe.' We sang it a few times before being overwhelmed by, what I can only describe as a numinous experience. It was as though time stood still and I, along with my friends, was caught up in an immense outpouring of love that filled our very souls. I remember being filled with such a sense of goodness and well being that I could not move.

Eventually, as the experience passed, we slowly became aware of ourselves and each other. I remember Tony saying, 'What just happened?' I looked at my watch and the whole afternoon had disappeared. We had been there for nearly three hours. Not a word had passed our lips since we stopped singing. Jane smiled and said, 'What happened? God happened.'

Over the last few years, two questions have monopolised my thinking. I am sure that they are right at the heart of the Scriptures. The two questions are, 'who am I and who are you?' It is hard to look at who we really are with our small-minded pettiness and it is hard to let God reveal Godself to us because that catapults us into an untidy messy place where we are not in control.

I think that is why most of us see the Scriptures as being about information rather than transformation when in fact the opposite is true. The Scriptures are inviting us to reflect on those two questions so that the work of the Spirit which is always to transform can begin. As long as you treat the Scriptures as sources of information then you will always be at a distance from what God wants to do. What is it that God wants to do? I think it is to tell us who we are and who God is.

I want to begin with the picture John paints of the person of Jesus. John is very much aware of the divinity of Christ. He is caught up in a numinous, mystical experience that he wants everyone to share in. He concentrates less on the humanity of Jesus than the other Gospels. For John, yes, Jesus is a human being, but Jesus is also divine. So, he preaches the Lordship of Jesus. He wants those who read the Gospel to make a personal act of faith in Jesus and, more than that, to enter into relationship with him so that his life becomes our life.

One of the Greek words that John uses is the word psyche which, I think, means the centre of a person's life where we feel our human emotions and desires and where we can begin to discover God. The thrust of the Gospel is to reflect, pray and ask God to help you discover who you are and who this God is. The invitation is to enter into the deepest part of you, that part that defies expression and discover God. It is a wonderful piece of writing.

Richard Rohr tells us in his book, 'Things Hidden: Scripture as Spirituality', that the word Gospel that we translate as Good News was a word taken from a culture where war and battles were accepted as the norm. A Gospel was a message of victory that announced a new beginning. These Scriptures are to so amaze us that we are to have a radical new beginning every time we read them. Can we really say that is true?

The new beginning John has to tell is about the love he himself has experienced. It was a love that was so deeply human and yet so divine that he declared Jesus to be the first truly human being who had ever walked the earth, the pioneer if you like of a new order of human society. He also saw that the love that had touched his life was the same love that had breathed the world and the universe into being and which held it together.

Somehow, in Jesus, John had come to know the source of everything that exists and discovered that this power of love is calling us to become what we truly are meant to be, living life to the full and experiencing that love. In a sense what happens is that we find in this love the reality of ourselves. Jean Vanier in his book on John's Gospel says, 'His healing and forgiving love called them forth to wholeness and to the discovery of how beautifully human and beautifully divine they were that they were beloved of God.'

Two other Greek words that are very important in John's Gospel are the words 'ano' and 'kato' which mean up and down. In a sense they are referring to two orders or patterns of living. In the kato order, the ruling principle is my ego, and the way in which it expresses itself in the world is through manipulation, competition and control. The ano order has as its ruling principle the spirit of love, and its expression is compassion, openness, sharing and vulnerability.

We all have both realities within ourselves. We are earthly and heavenly. We are sexual and spiritual. I guess true happiness depends on bringing them into harmony with each other, not allowing one to be submerged by the other. The truth is that, within most of us, kato rules and the ego is rife. That is why the world is in the state it is in.

In Jesus the two orders are reconciled. They are brought together and so in him we find perfect humanity and divinity. The Gospel invites us to realise that the consciousness of Jesus can be ours, that in each of us the ano and the kato can be reconciled.

I first met Alec in a retreat centre in the south of England. At first, he seemed shy and withdrawn, but when we began to speak, he opened up his soul and I discovered a man who was searching for God. He told me of his early life and his desperate attempts to escape his home in Manchester. He had been deeply scarred by his mother's suicide when he was eight and his father's subsequent alcoholism. After university, he took some time to travel in order to find himself. He told me that, while he was travelling, he tried many things to assuage the pain within him; sex, drugs and rock and roll were all part of his life.

He recognised that his journey at that time was very introspective. It was all about his needs and his desire to fulfil himself and find deep healing. He told me that he was manipulative and controlling of others in order to grab what was eluding him. Eventually he settled in a Buddhist monastery where he spent nearly three years. The silence and solitude comforted him within, and he began to find a modicum of peace.

He knew that, while he had discovered something, it was still all about him and his need. He sensed the call to a more whole life where others took a central place and so he left his Buddhist safe place and set off on a journey which eventually led him back to Manchester. It was there he became a worker for a small charity that helped with drug addicts. I met him in the retreat centre where he was taking some quiet before re-entering the fray. What I saw in him was a man who was in the process of reconciling the ano and the kato and it was a joy to see.

John uses completely different material to the synoptic Gospels, the origin of which we do not know. His material is written on at least two levels. Throughout the Gospel he writes on a physical level and on a spiritual level. It is this latter level that John is more interested in because at that level we discover our real self and the God who is within us.

He uses misunderstanding scenes to lead us from one level to the other. The scene with Nicodemus shows very clearly the different levels that the Gospel speaks at. Nicodemus asks at the human, physical level, 'How can a man be born again?' Jesus answers at a spiritual level. John invites us all the time to move to a deeper understanding.

He frequently uses words with more than one meaning; for example in the story of the crippled man cured at the pool of Siloam. The word 'Siloam' means sent. The whole story is a teaching on Discipleship. If you are not aware that the word has more than one meaning then the story of the man at the pool of Siloam is the story of the cure of a crippled man and nothing else.

All the time, while reading the Gospel you have to ask yourself the question, 'What does he mean?' The author of John's Gospel is not interested in truth, as we know it. As I have already said, in the Scriptures truth is far deeper than mere facts. Truth is about helping people understand the reality behind the incident or fact.

There are two words in Greek that mean time. The first is 'chronos,' which is indicative of a time-line for example, I was born in.... then I.... Then I.... John discards that. He is really not interested in what happened and the order in which it happened.

The second is 'kairos' which means the significance of the moment. John writes his Gospel to let us know the significance of the moments and he organises facts and puts into the mouth of Jesus the words that let us know the significance of the moment. The Gospel was written some years after the death of Jesus. Exact words and incidents cannot be remembered.

What is remembered is the significance of the moment and it is that which is inspired. It is that which has significance for us now. It is commonly held that John the beloved disciple wrote it, and if you read John 21: 23-24, he is identified as the witness behind the Gospel; but there is also mention of his death in 21: 20-23. It seems unlikely that he is the one and only author even though he may be responsible for much of the material used.

The message of the Gospel is very clear. Jesus is the Son of God who is the source of eternal life. Any good Jew would know, when reading the Gospel, what Jesus was saying when he begins his long monologues with 'I am'. In Jewish tradition only God can claim 'I am'. Go back to the Book of Exodus and you find God revealed as 'I am' to Moses in the story of the burning bush.

John is telling us that Jesus is God. The God who pre-existed time, the God who is always in the present. It is an incredible claim that spreads from the prologue to the end of the Gospel.

As if to reinforce who Jesus is, John shows how all the major Religious feasts have been replaced by Jesus. Jesus is now the one who reveals God. The Jewish background of symbolism, legalism and ritualism has been replaced by new Spiritual moments.

In chapter two, at the wedding feast of Cana we find the ritualism of purification replaced by the new wine of salvation which is, for John, the only reality that can really cleanse us and set us free.

In chapter three we find Jesus replacing the temple with his own body. That must have really scandalised the Jewish readers. The temple was the centre of their lives and here was this man telling them that it was no longer important, that only Jesus was important. What is John saying to us? Do not sink your hope in the material; do not build your Churches... It is the person of Jesus that matters. Have we really learnt the lesson?

Also, in chapter three, Jesus shows how birth into the chosen people is a spiritual reality dependent on God alone. In chapter four we find Jesus breaking down the Jewish provincialism, which said that God could only be worshipped in Jerusalem. In chapter five we begin the breaking down of the Jewish feasts. Jesus is the sabbath... we will only find rest in him. In chapter six he replaces the Passover saying, 'I am the bread of life'. It is all John's way of telling us that he is freedom, he is salvation. In chapter eight he declares himself the light of the world and the living water, replacing the symbolism used at the feast of tabernacles. In chapter ten, we find the feast of the dedication of the temple replaced, as Jesus himself is dedicated.

All the time he is moving Religion from the level of the institution to the level of the personal. I am the way, the truth and the life. 'Get to know Jesus', John is telling us, and you will understand that he is all the truth that matters. It is the personal all the time. I think we move away from the personal because the personal makes demands on us and makes us face reality. It is easier to live at the level of the institution.

You see, it is love that is the core of faith; nothing else; and I guess the biggest transformation or conversion, indeed whatever you want to call it, is in the realm of love. It is what circumcision of the heart is all about. In order to love, we have to change and that is not a comfortable challenge. It is the change that comes about through falling into grace. It is what God does within us.

Just recently I had lunch with a friend of mine who I sadly do not see as much of as I would like. Angela is an early retired teacher and she has allowed herself to fall into grace. When she was at work she had little time for God. She went to Mass on Sunday and read each month at the liturgy because that is 'what one did!' Then her sister died very suddenly from leukemia and Angela's neat, tidy world was shattered. Neither of them had married and spent the school holidays travelling together. They met at least once a week to eat and share together. They had no other relatives, so when her sister died, Angela fell apart. She was in a high-powered management job in school and decided to take early retirement. For months she stayed at home. I would visit, when in her part of the country, but there was little I, or anyone else, could do to ease her pain. From being a confident, outgoing person, she shrank into herself.

She still went along to Mass on a Sunday but no longer read. It was going into church one morning that things began to change. On the steps outside, she saw Jo, a homeless drunk. She offered her some money and Jo said 'No, tell me your story.' Jo had sensed the pain in Angela. As she looked at the woman, Angela felt something break inside her and all the pain locked inside burst out and she began to sob. Soon she found herself in the arms of this woman who held her.

When the tears subsided she felt differently. A little bit embarrassed, she hurried away from the church without going in and went home where she spent the day wondering what had happened. She knew that in the love of that homeless woman she had encountered the love of Jesus. She had begun to fall into grace and over the next years her heart and mind were completely taken over by love. She searched for Jo but never found her again. Her search led her to soup kitchens and night shelters and they became the focus of her life; now her whole identity is caught up in working for those in need. She never found Jo but is always immensely grateful to her for opening her heart to love.

Finally at the end of chapter ten, Jesus describes himself as the fullness of life. John seems to be saying to us, if you want life you will only find it in Jesus. A huge question to ask ourselves is whether or not we are aware of the call to a personal relationship with Jesus?

John's gospel is very cleverly structured to help us understand who Jesus is. It begins with the prologue in chapter1: 1-18. It was probably added after the rest of the gospel, an ancient hymn with additions. Some scholars now think a Christian community specifically wrote it. Whether or not it was John's community has not been confirmed by the scholars.

This is followed by the book of signs which runs from chapter 1:19 to chapter 12:50 and which culminates in the greatest sign of all, the raising of Lazarus from death. We then have the book of glory, chapter 13:1 - 20:31, in which John wanders around the mystery of who Jesus is and what he means. It is repetitive, frustrating and wonderful as John tries to capture the person of Jesus who can never be captured in words but really only experienced.

Finally, the Gospel concludes with the epilogue in chapter 21: 1-25 where the mystery of new beginning and forgiveness are all caught up in Jesus' encounter with the disciples on the shore of the sea of Galilee and his invitation to them to 'come and have breakfast'.

I am always attracted by people who have vision. Sometimes when we talk of visions and dreams, we think of supernatural occurrences like the visions and dreams we read about in the Bible. Visions and dreams can also be the ability to see the truth and to know that what you see can become a reality. That is the way that I think of dreams and visions today. People like Martin Luther King, Mother Teresa, and Oscar Romero can really catch hold of my imagination and tug at my heartstrings. They can speak to my spirit and bring a new experience of life somewhere deep within which is exhilarating and exciting.

One of the most beautiful things about people who have vision is that they love the world. I discovered this quotation from Frederick Buechner in his book 'Wishful Thinking'. 'A prophet's argument with the world is deep down a lover's quarrel. If they did not love the world, they probably would not bother to tell it that it is going to self-destruct. They would just let it go. Their quarrel is God's quarrel'.

People like the ones I have mentioned as well as hundreds of others believe that the world can be a good place to live, and I suppose that somewhere deep within myself I believe that too; so the vision they have touches that place of belief within me.

However, as they struggled to bring their dream to fruition, the reality of the lives of those people is very different. Martin Luther King struggled with weakness, was often pilloried and was on many occasions the victim of racial abuse. Ultimately his vision of a society of peace and harmony cost him his life. Mother Teresa must have been frightened to death to leave the relative comfort of the Loreto Sisters and begin to work with the poor on the streets of Calcutta. I am told that the Mother Teresa sisters each have only one habit. They do not even have the security of material goods. Oscar Romero's vision cost him his life as very slowly he began to stand against the oppressive regime that he lived in. To have a vision can be exciting, but to bring the vision to reality is very costly; and yet without such a vision the people will perish.

That was the reality for John the beloved Disciple. He had a vision that he could not let die. John had been so touched by Jesus, both human and divine, that he could not forget him, he could not walk away from him. Jesus was everything to John. He had become the all-encompassing focus of his life and John dreamed of the time that everyone would enter into the mystery of who Jesus is and begin to discover the heart of God.

As we read the Gospel, we find a depth and a beauty that no other literature has ever managed to capture. I have always asked myself why that was true; and it must be, because dreams and visions are born of the Spirit of God and inspired by the Spirit. So, the writings that we call John's Gospel are the same - touched, inspired, transformed by the Spirit.

John's dream is that through his writing, the reader knows who Jesus is, the only beloved son of God. He knows the truth that, without Jesus, life is meaningless and empty. Only Jesus can show us the way to true human fulfilment. Any other way only leads to emptiness and frustration. I was thinking just recently how much the world needs to hear again John's dream; a word of life in the midst of the death of anger bitterness and hatred; light in the darkness of abortion and warfare; water in the desert of starvation and famine. Jesus is the answer to the world's desire for peace and happiness, but that can only come about when people are convinced of who Jesus is.

John's Gospel is supposed to have been written for those who are already believers to help them deepen their awareness of Jesus. However, for the non-believer it can be a means to faith. I remember many years ago a young lad walked into a group I was leading in Dublin. He was covered in studs and chains, black leather from head to foot. He sat on the edge of the group never saying a word until suddenly completely out of the blue he launched into a tirade against everyone who was there. He told us that he had been abandoned by his parents as a baby. He was adopted into a family where he was beaten regularly. Eventually he had been thrown out on to the streets and was living in a squat. He was into the drug scene. After all that he said, 'how can you tell me that God loves me?' I had no idea what to do but after a couple of minutes of stunned silence I asked him to take away a copy of John's Gospel and read the passage that begins 'God so loved the World....' The next day he came back and shared how that night he had read the whole Gospel and suddenly had an insight into who Jesus is. It had changed his life and he wanted everyone to know what had happened to him. John's dream had caught him.

John wants us to know that we can make the dream real if we stay close to Jesus in prayer, if we enter into an intimate relationship with him. That is what all that beautiful writing is about where Jesus talks about the vine and the branches. If we remain in Jesus, we can love as he loved. It is not an impossible dream. John wants us to know we have the same privileges as Jesus the beloved Son, his Spirit lives within us. Through our Baptism and Confirmation, the same Spirit that inspired Jesus to do all that he did lives within us. We have his power, his authority to do even greater things than he has done, John tells us. Is that a challenge to open ourselves to divine love and let love flow through us? Sidney Carter once wrote, 'No revolution will come in time to alter this man's life except the one surprise of being loved.' Only love will change the world.

The world is hungry to know who Jesus is. The world is desperate for an answer to its craving for peace and fulfillment. Our lives can be key to the quest. We can show the world who Jesus is by love; love that is more than mere words but love which is action, and which touches the lives of those around us. Sometimes John tells us the world will not respond as we would want. There will be misunderstanding, we will get hurt but if we are caught up in John's dream that every one of God's Children knows the truth of who Jesus is then it is worth whatever we have to face. 'Be brave,' says Jesus. 'I have conquered the world.' Love has won the victory. I would like to close this chapter with a prayer of St Ignatius.

> Lord Jesus, teach me to be generous,
> to give and not to count the cost,
> to fight and not to heed the wounds,
> to work and not to seek for rest,
> save in the knowledge
> that we do your most holy will.

TWO

JESUS THE LAMB OF GOD

Just recently, I was having dinner with some friends. They told me the story of a young girl they had met. This young girl had severe drug and alcohol problems. Her name was Sarah and she came to my friends' attention when she burst into their solicitor's office looking for help. Sarah had a baby 12 months previously and the baby had been taken into care because of Sarah's problems. She was desperate to find a way of getting her child back.

My friends, Duncan and Lou, are family solicitors working in a poor part of the country, trying to help the disadvantaged. As you can imagine, they are not able to make a huge amount of money, but it is their faith that keeps them working in the area. They felt called by God to be there and they manage to get by.

Lou spent some time with Sarah and asked her if she could pray with her. Sarah readily agreed and started coming to see Lou regularly. The prayer went on and Lou and Duncan managed to get Sarah on to a rehabilitation programme. 12 months on and Sarah has supervised access to her child and if all goes well could in time be re-united with him.

What has excited Lou and Duncan more than anything is the change in Sarah. Faith has come to matter to her, and the prayer and the professional help has enabled her to re-discover her dignity. She moved away from the area that she had been living in and cut herself off from her former 'friends' who supplied her drugs. She enrolled in college to get some qualifications as a carer and became part of a local church. This young woman is once again excited about the future and the possibilities that she sees opening up before her. She has become a new creation, a radically different person than she was before.

You see, that new creation which Paul speaks of in his letter to the Galatians, can happen in us as we enter into the mystery of Jesus, both human and divine. A key word in John's Gospel is relationship. It is almost as though the author of the Gospel is saying to us, 'enter into relationship with Jesus, both human and divine and you will become a new person.'

What I would like to do in this second chapter on John's Gospel is look at the prologue of John's Gospel as the author unpacks for us who Jesus is. He makes it very clear that Jesus is the Son of God who pre-existed time and creation and that in him we come face to face with the reality of God.

We are very familiar with the opening words of John's Gospel, 'In the beginning was the word, the word was with God, and the word was God...' These opening words take us back to the book of Genesis. By alluding to the book of Genesis, John is declaring the beginning of a new creation. God saw that it was good, the original blessing of creation, the 'barak' of God, is being restored here. John wants us to know that Jesus is the fullest expression of

God who is eternally creative. He is very clearly stating that Jesus is divine.

The Greek for word is 'logos' which refers, not only to the spoken word but also to the idea and thought behind the spoken word. The word has the power to transform create and change; it is through the word that everything is created.

During the next two chapters we find a period of seven days taking place. This is to remind us of the creation of the world in seven days. We read about that in the book of Genesis. The author of John's Gospel shows us how Jesus is creating a new world order through the calling of the disciples into relationship with him.

I was recently working in a parish where I met a woman in her forties. She ran the Parish office, co-ordinated almost all of the catechetical programmes, helped to run the social outreach of the parish and was right at the centre of Parish life and activity. She was paid to work for twenty hours each week, but it looked as though she was doing at least fifty hours.

June was a charming person, for whom nothing was too much trouble. One day I sat having a coffee with her and she shared her story. She had been baptised Catholic but there her faith journey had come to an end, at least for a while. Her dad, who was the nominal Catholic, was alcoholic and life was tough. June left school at fifteen and went to work in a local solicitor's office. Her plan was to climb up the greasy pole and get away from home as soon as she could. She did very well and the solicitors she was working for saw her potential. By the time she was eighteen she was on day release at college, paid for her by her employers.

It was soon after that, June met Tony in a local pub. They started going out together and she was fascinated to discover that Tony was a person of faith. Pretty soon they were seeing each other regularly and June started going to Mass along with Tony. She said one Sunday, the Gospel was Matthew 25, the parable of the last judgement. June heard the Gospel inside herself and realised that much of her life was an empty sham. All she was concerned about was getting a good job which would provide for her materially and help her to live the high life. Deep inside herself she realised that she helped no-one and loved no-one other than herself. Even Tony was second on her list! She knew she had a lot of thinking to do and praying to do.

That led her to changing her life completely. She gave up her money-centred job, changed her attitude to life and entered into what she really saw as a new world order. Over the next few months, she became a Catholic and began to live for Christ. Her work in the church paid her a very small salary but it was more than that; it was a calling, a vocation that she had been given to walk alongside others and help them see more clearly.

The author of the Gospel goes on to tell us that the light is scattering the darkness of the old order. Something new is happening here. That 'something new' has to happen within us as well. As we welcome the light into our darkness, a new creation is taking place within us. Nothing can be the same again.

We enter into a new world order when we enter into relationship with this light, Jesus. It is because of Jesus that all is made new. Heaven and earth are no longer separate. Everything is holy because the light has shone. Holiness can be found in the ordinary that has been blessed and sanctified by the light that shines in the dark. The ordinary is made holy because the light has shone. It is amazing how easy we find it to divide and separate and refuse to believe that God is everywhere. It makes us small minded and petty. Sadly, that is how many Christians appear to those around us.

We are going to learn throughout the gospel that life is gift and that eternal life can be lived in the here and now as John writes, 'What has come into being in him was life... life that was the light of all...' That free gift of life, John tells us, brings enlightenment and cannot be overpowered by darkness. The great battle of good and evil is fought out within each one of us. If we choose to allow the life of the word to dominate, then darkness will never overpower it. I do not know what darkness is within you but let the light shine.

Prison ministry can be extremely rewarding, and while I do not have a prison ministry per se, I have been invited to preach to men in prison on lots of occasions and it is always a gift to me. I find myself marvelling at the presence of God that I always find and the way in which faith is somehow sustained in the hardest of situations. Just recently I was invited into a prison in the North of England to talk about mercy.

When I eventually got in, I met an extraordinary man called Peter. He came bouncing up to me as soon as I walked into the chapel. It seemed as though life was bubbling inside him. He reminded me a little of Tigger from the Winnie the Pooh stories as enthusiasm and energy flowed from him. He immediately began to share his experience of God with me. He had been in prison for many years and had been refused parole several times but, he told me, God had always been with him. He described how he came into the prison weighed down with his crimes, consumed by darkness and ready to take his own life. Through the ministry of another inmate who had encountered God, Peter's life changed. He said that as he learnt how to pray and to invite God into the darkness, it began to change until he realised the truth that he was never alone, that God lives within him. It changed his life as the darkness disappeared never to return. Light cannot be overpowered.

Verses 6-8 of chapter 1, are an addition to the prologue. If you take the verses out you find that the hymn continues as it was in the original. 'A man came sent by God. His name was John. He came as a witness, to bear witness to the light so that everyone might believe through him. He was not the light, he was to bear witness to the light.'

Light does not normally need a witness. If you put a light on, it speaks for itself, it illuminates. Yet John tells us that the light needed a witness because the eyes that were looking at the light were blind. It needed to be both heralded and announced.

This introduces us to another major theme that we will find in the gospel and that is the battle between the hostile world and the light of Jesus. The hostile world is represented by the Jews who refuse to believe when facing the light. Jesus will be shown as the victor over the darkness of unbelief. I think we face that battle between light and darkness in every aspect of life even in the Church.

John then speaks very powerfully when he says, 'the word was the real light that gives light to everyone; he was coming into the world. He was in the world that had come into being through him and the world did not recognise him...' The real light has come into the world. A light that is for everyone. That is what Peter had discovered.

Jesus, the messiah, has not come just for the Jews but for everyone. You see, the truth is that the light has shone indiscriminately. It has not shone on some and not on others, and we are not going to help people recognise it by deeming them unacceptable. I sometimes wonder how many more groups of people the Christian church can alienate; some groups of women, gay people, divorced and remarried people, those who have children outside marriage. The light is for all people, not just the comfortable middle class who say their prayers and sit in church on a Sunday. How has the light shone in your darkness?

Just recently I was at a showing of Jimmy McGovern's TV series 'Broken'. The showing was part of the parallel programme that took place at the Eucharistic congress in Liverpool in 2018. It is a very powerful series and well worth watching if you get the chance. It tells the story of Father Michael Kerrigan. He is the Parish priest of a large city centre parish in the north of England. He is very well-liked and well-respected. It seems as though everyone in the area knows him whatever their faith creed or colour.

Michael has lots of emotional baggage from his childhood. He grew up in a poor, working-class family and attended a strict, Catholic grammar school where he was abused. He struggles to maintain the mental and spiritual balance needed to serve parishioners and there are many moving scenes as Michael tries to cope with his own mental health. He also has to cope with his dying mother who is now completely dependent on others for her care. Michael has to try to make peace within himself with the hard, sometimes cruel, matriarch and the frail, weak and remorseful woman about to depart from this world.

With a widening caseload of personal problems, community conflicts and society's suspicions of the church at large, Michael begins to question just how much of an effect he can really have in the ever-evolving spiritual landscape of modern-day Britain.

That is the background to the series which I have borrowed from Jimmy McGovern's synopsis on the series. The episode we watched was the encounter between a gay man and a black man whose nephew has died in tragic circumstances. He has come to support his sister from Trinidad. The other man is his sister's neighbour and friend. The man from Trinidad could not cope with the other man's presence. It is a wonderful exposition of the way in which we blame and scapegoat one another for the flimsiest of reasons. After the showing and the silence that followed it, Jimmy McGovern and the script writer who had written that episode took questions. The script writer who was with Jimmy was gay and he shared how that episode had been based on the story of a friend of his who had eventually taken his own life because of the prejudice that he had experienced.

By the end of the session many people were in tears. Afterwards I went up to the young man and asked for forgiveness for the ways in which the Church had hurt him and those of his friends. He was extraordinarily gracious, and as he hugged me, he said that the Church might not understand but he knew that God did. He told me that he was not bitter towards the Church in any way or even angry. He said that at times he was just sad. It was so moving that this young man could find a way of living with the Church's teaching without recourse to anger and bitterness, but also he knew the truth that God understands. The light had shone. Those who were able to respond to the light, John tells us, he gave power to become children of God. The children of God are born of God. I mentioned in the last chapter about the different levels the gospel is written on. Those who recognise the light learn to live in a different way, in the power of love, living lives of forgiveness and peace. That is what we are called to do. The light has shone. Those who live in that light are to reflect the life of God for the world, a life of love that would conquer everything that stops us from understanding the things of God.

John then tells us that those who recognise the light begin to discover that the father of Jesus is the God of Israel, the father of the world and we, as children, are called to relate to God in the same way as Jesus did. We are to enter into relationship with the divine, present in the human person of Jesus. That relationship is to be a parent/child relationship, so close that we know our very being comes from God.

We then reach the climax of the prologue when we read those words that at Christmas time, often roll glibly off our tongues 'the word became flesh, he lived among us and we saw his glory, the glory that he has from the father as the only son of the father, full of grace and truth.'

The word became flesh and lived among us. Jean Vanier says Jesus became a pilgrim and a brother walking through the desert with us. That is the most incredible statement that John could make. The one who pre-existed time, through whom everything has life, has not just entered humanity but became flesh and took his place in human history. We can enter into relationship with him.

We translate the Greek into 'he lived among us', but apparently the pure Greek translation is 'he pitched his tent'. He lived as we did. In the first testament, in the book of Exodus, God asked Moses to make him a dwelling among his people and that became the focus of God's presence for them. The people were free to walk in and out and bask in the glory of God. Jesus has become the new tent where people could meet God and find life and rest.

God is no longer distant or set apart from the world. If only we could believe that. The ancient peoples saw their Gods as being scarily apart and ruling over their creation. We suffer at times from their legacy. It is why we have to become a new creation. We have to let go of the images of God that are unhealthy and often based in folklore rather than experience. God has chosen to become one with us. In God there is communion, unity, love and light. Relationship with the God who created everything is ours. We only have to open ourselves to it.

Verse 15 is another addition about the mission of John the Baptist and then we move into the final verses of the prologue. It is there we read 'indeed from his fullness, we have all of us received - one gift replacing another, for the law was given through Moses, grace and truth have come through Jesus Christ. No-one has ever seen God; it is the only son who is close to the father's heart, who has made him known.'

Jesus contains within himself the fullness of God. Frances Hogan in her book 'John the beloved disciple says, 'All that come from him comes as an overflowing fountain, one gift after another. The Jews regard the gift of the law given through Moses as the greatest gift that they could possibly receive, but that gift has been surpassed in Jesus. In Jesus God, is showing us his abundant life and love bringing about the new covenant. All of us have received unconditional free love.'

As soon as the prologue finishes, we have the introduction of John the Baptist's testimony to Jesus. I guess, in many senses, the

Baptist reminds us that we are all called to be witnesses to the coming messiah through the lives we live. John the Baptist invites us to discover more about the theme of relationship as he witnesses to Jesus and encourages his own disciples to follow the Lord.

It is John the Baptist who makes the first positive statement of who Jesus is in chapter 1:29 when he says, 'look there is the lamb of God who takes away the sin of the world'. I know that I have written about this before, but that phrase is loaded with symbolism and worth reflecting on again as the author of the Gospel reminds us that Jesus has come from God and is God. To name Jesus as the 'lamb of God' is shocking and should radically alter our perception of who God might be. John invites us to get rid of our theological and philosophical concepts and to allow God to reveal Godself to us. It is so frightening to say, 'I do not know, and I do not understand.' As Church we have not been good at admitting our vulnerability. Nor have we been honest enough to say that we are only ever discovering. After all, there is always more in God. Even the attempts to put language on that which we do discover is only ever scratching the surface of the truth we are trying to convey.

The author seems to want us to know that the experience of Jesus shows us a vulnerable God, a God who is ultimately broken and weak, a God who suffers, a God who is a lamb. The title evokes a whole series of meanings. The suffering servant is described by Isaiah as a lamb, who bears the sins of the world. The blood of the lamb had protected the Israelites in Egypt. During the

Passover the lamb is sacrificial and would evoke images of the liberation from bondage.

Because we do not understand the imagery, it does not allow the shock value of what John was saying to really break through. The lamb for the Jew was dirty, weak and ordinary, and John says, 'look there is the lamb of God.' Can you imagine what that must have done to any God-fearing Jew?

John the Baptist goes on to say to us that entering into relationship with God is possible because the lamb will take away the sin of the world. Note that sin is singular. In John's gospel, there is only one sin and that is not to believe that you are a son or a daughter of God. It is all about relationship.

Everything we are that stops us knowing who we are in God's sight is going to be dealt with by the sacrificial lamb. All our poor self-image, shame and pettiness is taken on by him. If we see at all, then we will see it die in the naked vulnerability that is the lamb of God. Everything that takes away our dignity and stops us believing that we are beloved children of God will be raised and transformed into newness of life. It is that broken, bruised body that opens the way into relationship with God. If that does not blow your mind about who God is, then nothing will.

John's gospel is all about process and the process of relationships, and so Jesus says to the two disciples in answer to their question, 'where do you live?' to 'come and see.' It is as if he is saying 'come and discover who I am, come and see what I have to offer.' He does not teach them academically but invites them to share with him.

The Greek word 'menein' which means 'to stay or dwell' is used 63 times in John's gospel and the letters which are given his name. It is used it to signify the sort of intimacy that God wants with us, that dynamic intimate involvement with another person. You know, God delights in us and all we can do in response is enjoy it, but sadly most of us do not enjoy it. We question it, we doubt it, anything but accept it.

The disciples were never quite the same again. One of them was Andrew, maybe the other is meant to be us. Somehow that phrase, the lamb of God, becomes a reality for them. This Jesus takes on, their pain. He encourages them to become something else, other than their pain. It changes Andrew so much that he goes to Peter and says, 'We have found the messiah.' Peter then meets Jesus and when Jesus looks at him, he does not just see brokenness and pain. He sees what Peter, and indeed each one of us, can become through the power of sacrificial love.

When they have begun to discover, they go and tell others. It is a valuable lesson to learn that disciples make disciples. We can put on all the courses in the world but that will not make disciples.

The moment the disciples respond to the lamb their journey in faith begins and the mystery of Jesus unfolds and we, the reader, go with them on their journey. By the end of the gospel, we can say with Thomas, 'My Lord and my God'.

Unlike the Synoptic Gospels, John does not mention all of the twelve apostles in this section. He is interested only in giving us a summary of what they discovered about Jesus and in preparing us for his revelation, through his signs, that he is the Son of God who wants to bring us life and calls us to intimacy with him.

THREE

SEARCHING FOR GOD

One of my closest friends was a priest called Steve, about whom I have written before. He was a gifted, creative man, full of fun and with an ability to relate to people that was second to none. When he arrived on the staff at the seminary where I was training, he was 29, just a few years older than me, and we hit it off immediately. We used to talk until late at night and I slowly got to know him well.

He loved people, and was fascinated by humanity. He loved God and was overwhelmed and fascinated by God's presence in his life. He loved the Gospel and spent a lot of time praying and reflecting on the Word of God. He had little time for rules and regulations that imprisoned people and was constantly doing all he could to set people free within themselves. As the years went by, we grew closer and closer, and I have to say he had a profound influence on me.

He was one of those wonderful priests who fell in love and, after a lot of soul searching, left the active ministry, married and had a beautiful family. He never saw himself as anything but a priest, albeit a married one, and I have often wondered why the Church is unable to allow him, and countless others, to continue in their priestly ministry. Sadly, he died in his early fifties from a heart condition and when his wife phoned me to tell me that news, I knew that I had lost someone very special.

I used to go with him when he was filling in for priests who were on holiday or who needed a break. One particular weekend, we drove from Durham to Alnwick in Northumberland. We arrived early in the afternoon and, after a walk around the town, got ready for the Saturday evening Mass. When it came to the homily, Steve stepped down off the sanctuary and began to wander up and down the Church. Every now and then he would stop and look at some one and smile and say to them, 'Do you know that you are loved by God?' Several people had tears in their eyes as Steve sat down next to them and held their hands for a moment or put his arm around them explaining that God was as close to them as he, Steve, was. It was a very powerful image of entering into the mystery that is God, of being held by a God who can only love.

I often reflect on that experience and have wondered why people found it so moving. I think it is because it suggests what is true, that there is an intimate relationship between God and humanity. When you touch another person, you are touching God and when another person is touching you, they are touching God. I think that searching for God demands an openness to humanity, for God is in the human condition, present in good and bad alike. I think one of our problems is that all too often we divorce the spiritual from the human and never the twain shall meet. John recognises the wonderful truth that the word has become flesh and lives among us. God is present in the human making it holy and sacred. Open your eyes and see. Search for God in the mundane and recognise God's presence in what is deeply and profoundly human. Search for what it means to be fully human, and you will find God. Do not divorce one from another. Find the depth of forgiveness within yourself, and you will find God. Find the depth of passion within yourself, and you will find God. God is there and will lead you ever more deeply into the wonder that is yourself, and the wonder that is God. Do not live at the superficial level that the world invites you to live at: running away from pain, blaming others, and judging others, so that you do not have to face yourself; possessing money, power, knowledge so that you do not have to begin to understand yourself. When, in John's Gospel, Jesus prays for his Disciples he prays that they be kept safe from the world. It is that he wants us to be kept safe from the false understanding of humanity that the world would have us accept, so that we can enter into a truer understanding of what it means to be a human being. It is in the searching that we discover God's presence.

What happens when we enter into this deeper understanding of the relationship between God and humanity? We look without condemnation at the mystery of ourselves and learn to make friends with ourselves and with the God who is present in us. We have to make friends with all the parts of ourselves that we have hidden away if we are to make friends with the God who is present in them. On my own journey I had to make friends again with the little boy who loved flowers and music and art rather than push him away and blame him for the relationship I had with my father.

It is when we begin to go on that journey of discovery that we experience the true inner freedom that God wants us to experience. When we make friends with ourselves and no longer have to judge or blame others for our hurts or our pain then we know we are free. When we know that our desire for the material is no longer necessary, and that poverty is not to be feared, then we are free. When our security lies in discovering who we are, and in discovering God is present in us, then we begin to discern what is important in life. The number of people who think life depends on what they own, particularly in our western culture, is amazing. One of the most beautiful and challenging things for me about my mum's dying came when I watched her going around her home and deciding where her possessions were going. They no longer mattered, and it was a real letting go. All that life depends on is discovering the God who is present in the human condition. Search for it and be faithful to that reality because there is nothing else that lasts eternally. The Gospel has to happen within us before it can begin to happen around us. We have to be on the journey of discovering the incarnate God if we are to be authentic witnesses to the reality of God's presence. The only authentic witness is someone who is on the journey not someone who has simply heard about the journey.

Then we will proclaim a truth to live by to the world, which has such credence to it that it will scare those whose trust is elsewhere. The world can cope with a Christianity that invites people to go to Church and still live in the world with all its selfishness and sin. It cannot, and will not, cope with a Christianity that invites people into discovering the truth and beauty of humanity. The challenge is too great if it is delivered by an authentic witness. That is why Jesus was crucified. The only authentic witness to the beauty of humanity and divinity and the world could not handle it because it involves letting go of all the trappings, we carry around with us. That is freedom and it is a scary place to be, but it brings life.

It seems to me, then, that the Jesus way is the only way to life and that his way is somehow discovering the beauty within and, in that beauty, the God who is present. That might be a painful journey, but experience shows that life very often comes from pain. One of the most beautiful passages in John's Gospel is one of the resurrection passages when Jesus appears to his Disciples and shows them his hands and his feet. It is extraordinary to know that the risen Jesus is still the wounded Jesus. We do not walk into life without our wounds; we walk into life having made friends with them so that they no longer control us, and we trust in the God whose presence we have discovered in our brokenness. We trust that God will be God.

I think that John was very much aware of the truth that God is as close to us as the very air that we breathe. He was filled with the knowledge that the human and the divine are intimately connected. He had seen, touched, tasted, and experienced that reality in Jesus and wanted us to do the same. He wanted us to enter into a mystery that can consume us and invigorate us, but a mystery that we can never come to the end of. As I hope I have shared in the last two chapters, John was very much aware not only of the divine nature of Christ but also of the truth of his humanity and he saw in Jesus an icon of humanity, in that, if we search for God we will experience God as Jesus did, mutually abiding, one within the other.

The whole of chapter fifteen of John's Gospel is all about communion. It is about what it means to be present to another, to remain with another. It speaks of friendship, real friendship, and of that mutual indwelling that has been focused on throughout the Gospel. It both invites and challenges us to take the risk of intimacy, of knowing and being known, of being vulnerable and weak with God and therefore with other people. In his daily meditation, Richard Rohr says, 'If you cannot honour the divine indwelling, the presence of the Holy Spirit, within yourself, how could you see it in anybody else? You cannot. Like knows like. All awareness, enlightenment, aliveness, and transformation begins with recognising that your own eternal DNA is both divine and unearned; only then are you ready to see it everywhere else too. Soul recognises soul.'

Mystery is impossible to penetrate, or it would not be a mystery, so while we can never exhaust the depths of God, I think it is true to say we can search for and experience God. We can enter into relationship with God. That is why the word relationship is so important in John's Gospel. We find John stating often that real life only comes through knowing Jesus in the intimate way that the word knowing meant for the Hebrews. It really is all about relationship. If only we would believe that life comes through knowing Jesus and that we are invited to enter into the glory of the family of God, to allow God to possess us and envelop us so that we can find life, love and peace.

What John seems to be reminding us in his Gospel is that we can experience relationship with a God who is always creating. Whether in Genesis or in John, God breathes life into the world and into us. The God in whom every creative thought and action has its origin is open to us and to relationship with us. This incredible creative power, the source of all that is, wants to know us and to love us; and more than that, wants to continue creating within us and through us. Take time to savour creation. Climb a mountain. Marvel at the majestic nature of a tree. Look at the fragility and beauty of a flower until it brings tears to your eyes. Be filled with delight at the intricacies of the human person. Rejoice in the moment without worrying about the past or the future. Delight in yourself for you are fearfully and wonderfully made.

When I was a child, I used to go to Anglesey, in Wales, to stay on a farm. It was owned by the son of a friend of my mum who would take us there for the weekend. I absolutely loved it. The air seemed so much fresher than where we lived and the animals and the dirt and the mess so much more real. I loved walking across fields and watching sheep give birth. I would stand for hours watching the pigs snuffling around their sty. I watched the ducks and the geese on the farmyard pond and laughed at their clumsiness on the ground and their elegance on the water. I loved the home-made bread, butter and cheese. When it was raining there was nothing better than to sit in the farm kitchen in front of the range and eat bread and dripping. I felt close to all that was good and wholesome when on the farm. It seemed to ground me in reality. I used to spend a lot of time when I was there with a farmworker called Hughie. He was not the most articulate of men. Indeed, it seemed at times that he had nothing to say. However, every now and then he would reveal some powerful wisdom. One day I was helping him feed some pigs and he looked at me and smiled and said, 'This is as close to God as you will ever get.' Then he carried on doing what he was doing, and I suddenly saw a man who, in the midst of God's creation, was experiencing all that mattered and all that was important. God!

We can experience relationship with a saving God. John reveals Jesus as the God who saves us if we only care to open ourselves to relationship with that God. This all-powerful creative God has become flesh in Jesus and through that becoming, has opened the way to life that knows no end. What is it that we are saved from? I know there are very clever theological arguments about Jesus' death on the cross and what that means for humanity. I do not think that to be saved is just about going to heaven when we die. It has to have something to do with living now, knowing the truth that you are loved by God, that you do not deserve it, that you cannot earn it and that love is poured out for you constantly. It is about knowing the truth of the Lamb of God and the truth of God's sacrificial love that heals and transforms us. It changes everything; the way you think, the way you act, but I think chiefly we are saved from ourselves and the mess of our lives. Our relationship with Jesus means we do not have to be sucked into the morass that is all around us, but can live in peace and harmony with ourselves and with others.

My uncle Lol was a charming, suave man with a hint of danger about him. He was one of those people that we called uncle even though there were no blood ties between us. He was married to aunty Edith. Both Edith and Lol had grown up with my mum and her brother and sister. They were part of a wide circle of young people who played tennis together and socialised around St Hugh's Church in Liverpool. Lol had always held a candle for my aunty May who very sadly died of TB when she was in her early twenties. Edith was May's best friend and mum often said that it was when May died that Lol found the person he should really have been with. He was a teacher and played the organ at St Hugh's for many years until he died.

I remember mum telling me that Lol had a fierce temper when he was young, so much so that many people were frightened of him. Maybe that was the danger that I sensed in him. He could be very sarcastic and cut people dead even with a look. He realised that he needed to change and so he began to pray every day that God would change him, soften his heart and enable him to be gentle and kind. God heard his prayer and over the years, as he opened himself to God, that change began to happen within him. Slowly but surely Lol was saved from himself and others were saved from his caustic tongue!

Then we have the Spirit, an indwelling God who leads us into the truth of relationship with God, of intimacy with God. Somehow, the very essence of who God is comes to live within us if we want to experience that, and that essence of God will lead us to the truth that we only find ourselves in and through God. It is extraordinary to think that by the Spirit we have become the dwelling place of God. Sadly, most of us do not really believe that truth, that we are god bearers for the world. It says something about the authority of experience as against head knowledge. We have to trust our experience of the indwelling Spirit just as the early church communities were aware of their own experience of the Spirit's presence. We are really not very good at trusting our own experience. In my Catholic tradition, we rely too much on what Father tells us, or Sister tells us. Yet our experience of the indwelling Spirit is just as valid and sometimes more so. We have to trust our experience and learn how to share it with others. Very few of us recognise the Spirit living within us and yet without that Spirit we simply exist, let alone live.

One of my friends is a poet and artist called John. He is a wonderfully mercurial person. He does not own a car, a mobile phone or a computer. He lives very simply in a small terraced house with a couple of other people who think in the same way as he does, at least about material things! It is very difficult to tie him down and make arrangements with him because he sees no need for a diary or a watch. He always surprises me with his ability to be in the present moment. When I call to see him, and he is in the house, it is as though he only has that moment and it is shared with me. I have had cards from him written in different parts of the world when I have expected him to be at home, but he has simply taken himself off to travel. He is very bright and sees things in an unusual way which can be frustrating at times. I was sharing with him one day some of my frustrations in life. He listened long and hard and then he said to me, 'Listen to your guts because that is where you will find God and then you will know what to do.'

The Spirit is within and I think John's advice to me to listen to my guts has been a lesson in discernment. The Spirit is within us and if we can just take the time to be still and to really listen, then we will recognise the promptings of the Spirit and hear the voice of God. We will know relationship with this indwelling God.

What is the key to experiencing and opening up to relationship? I think that it is time spent gazing at God and trusting that God is gazing upon us and, more than that, delighting in us. God is fiercely in love with us with a passion and an intensity which is almost frightening. I guess that is why we run away from God so much. We cannot cope with the intensity. If you do not believe me read the Song of Songs in the first Testament. Some of the songs and imagery would make a navvy blush but it expresses a love that is the most incredibly strong reality. God is our lover with the single-minded delight that a lover has for the loved one. It is that truth that makes Paul break out in song in the letter to the Romans in chapter 8 and say that there is nothing, absolutely nothing, that can separate us from the love of God. No sin, no hard-heartedness, no evil, no poor self-image; nothing can separate us from the love of God. This same God not only loves us, but actually likes us. God wants to be with us just to while away the hours. God enjoys our company. God delights in us.

That means our life with God is not just about saying prayers, filling the space with empty words which make us feel good about having done our duty. It is not about words that are meant to appease a God who demands that we pray. It is certainly not so that we can get into heaven or avoid hell. It is simply being in the presence of God because God is God, and in God, there is real life, rich vibrant, pulsating life.

That entering into relationship suggests that there is another way of living than the world's rather sterile, one-dimensional understanding where all that matters is me and my fulfilment. It is an unconventional way of living that becomes a dance of love with God where we enter into the rhythm and dynamism of the trinity and the life that is shared there. Our understanding of God as a trinity of persons is all about mutuality and abiding love.

Entering into that reality means that we come to see completely differently than we might have done otherwise. There is a heightened awareness of the presence of God everywhere, even in those moments and people we would rather run from. That implies an openness and a sensitivity to everything around us. It implies that we take time to savour and contemplate the gift of creation and each other so that we can see more clearly. That relationship means that we slowly free ourselves in the power of God from judging and blaming and scapegoating which seem to be the tenets on which the world exists. We live with a sense of joy in the sheer gift of being alive. Hildegard of Bingen was a saint, composer and poet but it is really only relatively recently that her songs, writings, and remarkable life and visions have been re-discovered. She was born over 900 years ago, and for most of her life was shut away in an obscure Benedictine monastery in the Rhineland. She once wrote, 'I am the fiery life of the essence of God; I am the flame above the beauty in the fields; I shine in the waters; I burn in the sun, the moon, and the stars. And with the airy wind, I quicken all things vitally by an unseen, all-sustaining life.' When we enter in relationship with this God, it seems as though we become the very presence of God for the world, and it is then that contemplation becomes a way of life. Richard Rohr says, 'I do not like to think of it so much as something you do but something you are, so I often use the phrase - the contemplative stance. It is a way of living, moving, and being in this world.'

So it seems that the invitation John is giving us is to open ourselves to the reality of God and experience the life-giving presence of God who is life giver, saviour and indweller, and the more we open ourselves to God the more we will recognise God all around us. It is about living with a heightened awareness that sees with eyes that are not clouded. That is why it is so important that we let our creator love us, Jesus free us, and the Spirit fill us because that unblocks our eyes and helps us to see. The challenge of the Jesus John reveals to us, is to enter into a deep intimate relationship with him and meet the God that he reveals.

FOUR

GENTLE JESUS MEEK AND MILD
(really?)

I was about 19 when I first heard about the 'monk in the woods.' I was taken along to Mass at Ince Benet monastery. It was here that Tom Cullinan, a Benedictine monk, had begun to establish a type of monastic life in the woodland around the village of Ince Blundell. Ince Blundell is an ancient settlement which lies between Liverpool and Southport. I was fascinated by this man who, in many ways, was so caught up with the gospel of Christ that he became a radical proponent of it. As I listened to him over the years, I was struck by his commitment, his profound wisdom and his simplicity. At Ince Benet he maintained a rhythm of prayer, work and study for many years and just invited others to join him.

Tom had arrived in the Archdiocese of Liverpool to establish a small monastic house with two other monks. They settled at first in a converted coach house at Little Crosby where they lived simply without the pressure of a parish or school. Tom was often asked, 'What is this about?' or, 'What are you doing?' He would smile and respond by asking why did the questioner really need to know? I guess he was challenging his questioners not to be defined by their role or their purpose but simply to be, which is always the hardest thing to discover. I remember my friend David Wells telling me that, when he moved to Devon, he went to his local pub for the first time. He got chatting and a man asked him,

'What do you do?' David thought for a while and then in his own inimitable style said, 'Well sometimes I swing naked from the light bulbs. What do you do?'

The monks were doing very ordinary things; cooking, gardening, cleaning, binding books, writing, earning their keep. Most importantly, they were trying to create space to find God in the ordinariness of life and to reflect on their experience. During this time, work began on building Ince Benet. By the time it was finished, Tom was the only monk left. For a variety of reasons, the others had gone back to the monastery. Tom's initial vision of a house for monks living a simple life and open for people to share, was now developed by him and those who shared his vision and understanding of the Gospel.

It was at Ince Benet, over many years, that Tom continued to respond to issues of social justice and the environment. He wrote and was often invited to speak at conferences, nationally and internationally. He also maintained that wonderful Benedictine hospitality, welcoming visitors from far and wide. His soup was legendary! Tom was never really understood by those who were his superiors. He was often seen by the more orthodox as radical and a bit odd. He was a wonderful man who at times could make others uncomfortable with his wisdom, insight and directness. For me he was a real prophet as he lived his simple, ordinary life of work, prayer and reflection and challenged others to look again at their own lifestyles.

I think it is true that if we follow Jesus, we will be both

misunderstood and seen as strange. Richard Rohr, when reflecting on Mark's Gospel, makes a very clear point about the Jesus that Mark presents to us. It seems that he is very much misunderstood. In chapter 3: 20-21, we are told that not even his own family understood him. So much so, that his relatives, whoever they may have been, decided he was crazy and set out to capture him.

It is quite obvious that Jesus was not very proper. He did things and said things that even his family were embarrassed by. He made himself unclean, in the traditional Jewish understanding, by the people that he mixed with and ate with. He was certainly not the sort of bland, insipid, nice person, doing all the right things, that we normally associate with religious people.

Maybe that is telling us that our very concept of religion has somehow become skewed. We think that purity, particularly sexual purity, is the be all and end all of religion, rather than living like the radical founder of Christianity and the Gospel he proclaimed. He was outside the mainstream, a wild radical preacher that even his family thought crazy. Rohr then makes the point that 'Religion is not doing nice, right, ordinary things that humans expect. God's goodness strikes much deeper than that and demands much more.' Most of us ignore that truth.

Mark's Jesus certainly did not fulfil the image that many of us have of the Lord. He is not a white European, with a simpering smile and greasy ringlets hanging down to his shoulders. He is an extreme activist who, at all costs, sought to be true to the love of God and to speak that truth to the world. I often look at the pronouncements that we, as Church, make and ask myself, are we seeking to be true to the love of God? Or are we simply seeking to be true to a system and a bureaucracy that seems at times to be a long way removed from the Gospel of Christ? Rohr says of Jesus' preaching, 'The world did not want to hear it. He would be crucified again today, and maybe even by the Church.'

I think it would be fair to say that the gospel Mark's Jesus proclaims cannot be forced into the parameters that we want it to fit into. Jesus took risks to be faithful to love, mercy, justice and truth. Sometimes we have to take risks to proclaim the Good News and often what we do will not be seen as acceptable or even orthodox. However, whose approval are we looking for? Jesus looked for no-one's approval. I think it's really difficult for us to understand the Jewish culture of the day. Tradition held that to exclude the poor and the sinner and the tax collector was the right and moral thing to do. Their sin had separated them from God. They had broken the covenant. If the Jews sat and ate with sinners, then they too would break that covenant and bring the wrath of God down on their heads.

This was not just a crazy Rabbi being nice to people. This was a threat to the covenant and ultimately to the whole existence of Israel as a nation which was based on the covenant. Peter McVerry, a Jesuit priest, has written a book called, 'Jesus, Social Revolutionary' and in it he wrote this, 'Only one man, Caiaphas, understood the significance of what Jesus was doing when he said it is better for one man to die than the nation perish.' Jesus eating with tax collectors and sinners was a profoundly political act as he revealed the face of God.

I often think that we keep Jesus locked up and safe. We keep him in the arena of piety and devotion. This man who is supremely free, filled with the wildness of the Spirit, who knows no guile in the way he acts or responds to people and we try to tame him and domesticate him.

I think we tame Jesus because he is the model for what we are supposed to be, and if we can keep him safe and respectable, all the better for us. Yet he is the supremely free person who, in his humanity, having had a life changing experience of God in the desert, lived as the son of God. He did this to show us how we are to live as sons and daughters of God.

One of my heroes was the great author, speaker and retreat giver, Daniel O'Leary. I used to meet him occasionally in a coffee shop, not too far from where I live. Daniel was blessed with far seeing eyes and was never frightened of pushing theological boundaries in order to try and understand what it meant to live as a child of God. He loved people and their stories and was a man of great compassion. The last time I saw him, before he died, he told me that finding God was the only thing that mattered and the place we would find God was in the midst of humanity. What truth he spoke; but we would rather look for the extraordinary than the ordinary to find God.

Just recently I was working with a group of people who were quite shocked when I said that the gospels are not biographies of Jesus or chronologies of what really happened. Mark is not interested in fact as we understand it. His community are not even asking the questions, 'Is that what really happened' or, 'Did it happen in that order and in that chronological framework?' He is interested in something far deeper. He is interested in what the passion, death and resurrection means for those who say they follow Jesus. For some reason, most of us seem to need to have a strict biography of Jesus, to tell us what he really did and how he really did it and when it happened. I think, in many cases, we are asking the wrong questions and we force the evangelist to meet our needs. Mark is not concerned with giving us a biography of Jesus. He is concerned, not with giving us a series of prescriptions and doctrines and dogmas by which all people must be saved for all time, but he is interested in giving you a description of a person who has saved them and freed them and loved them. For Mark, that Jesus, is not safe and comfortable but radical and open and always willing to challenge the perceived assumptions of his day. Many of us find that difficult to handle, which is why we sometimes find it easier to create a Jesus we can handle.

The Gospels are, in great part, a gathering together of that kind of deeply felt and understood relationship. So, I would ask you in reading the Gospel to examine the relationships going on. What is happening between Jesus and the people he encounters? Why would Jesus be saying this word to that person and why would the person answer back in that way? What is the gaze of God that is passing between that brother and sister, between Jesus and the blind man or the leper? That is how we get an insight into Mark's Jesus and it is clear that Mark's Jesus is a very human person who has little concern for the social niceties of his day, whatever they may be.

One of my friends, John, died several years ago and I still miss him greatly. He had a wonderfully irreverent sense of humour. He was never predictable and was seldom bothered by the expectations of others. He was warm and very human but at times he would make me shake my head as he opened his mouth and said the first thing that came out of his mouth. Often this was hilarious and sometimes very hard hitting.

I remember him standing up for the parish where he was priest. The school and parish were both headed for closure and John, at the cost of his mental health, took on the authorities and stood alongside his people. He was threatened in all sorts of ways, but he was faithful to those people with whom he shared his life and unconcerned about what was the proper thing to do.

Please, do try not to come to the Gospels presuming that we know what Jesus is supposed to do, or even what he is trying to do. Sadly, we all have our assumptions and our agendas. If we want to meet Mark's Jesus and let this word be a word of power, we need to let it speak without our western 21st century impositions; without our interpretations of truth and fact and history.

What I would like to do now is to look at an overview of Mark's Gospel, maybe picking out some of his major themes that will then give us an insight into this Jesus, as Mark has discovered him. Mark's is the simplest and the shortest gospel. It is largely a passion narrative pointing us towards Jesus' crucifixion and the understanding of that crucifixion. The cross stands at the heart of this Gospel. What we can say for certain is that the author wants to prove to his community that Jesus is the Messiah, the anointed one.

Mark also wants us to see Jesus as the suffering servant who comes to the full knowledge of who he is, through the cross. He comes to his glory in an absurd and backward way, the way of the cross. Mark constantly emphasises Jesus as the suffering servant.

It seems that Mark does not want his reader to proclaim that Jesus is Lord too quickly or too lightly. For Mark, we are invited to really understand what we are saying and its implications, because to say we follow him implies that, like Jesus we are willing to go through darkness to find light. It means that we are prepared to go through suffering and death to find life. Most of us really do not understand what is being asked of us. Mark, in painting a picture of a wild, free, intensely human person who suffers and discovers through darkness who he is, is inviting us to know that following this man Jesus is never going to be easy. This is not the sugar-coated Gospel.

As a Church we have historically been interested to prove that Jesus was God. Certainly, as theology developed and great councils of the church like Ephesus and Nicaea began to take place, the question of the divinity of Christ was of major importance. Very sadly, we got caught in that proof-test mentality, to prove to people that Jesus was God. Yet it seems that Jesus, in his own lifetime, did not seem preoccupied with that. In fact, the risk that Jesus took was the risk of looking normal. It was the risk of looking ordinary, the risk of being human. It was the risk of showing the love of God in, and for, a messy, dirty, broken world.

I often think that the great risk God took in Jesus, the risk of being human, has been the risk that the church has always been afraid to take. So in our art and our sculpture and in our teaching, we have stressed Christ's divinity with little thought of his humanity We have been afraid that if we were not able to powerfully, logically, philosophically prove to people that Jesus was God and to show that he really works miracles and that his state is divine, then people would not believe. We did not understand the way of the suffering servant. The backward, upside down way by which we come to God. It is not philosophical proof that leads us to Jesus but the lived experience of the Jesus way. That is what Mark is trying to show us and tell us in the Jesus he reveals.

The vital technique that Mark's Jesus seems to use is called the messianic secret. Again and again, after Jesus performs a miracle, we find the same line at the end, 'Do not tell anybody.' Mark is trying to help us to recognise that we will not come to understand what God is doing on earth or who God is, from signs and wonders. The way to understand is to follow, to walk the Jesus way. So, he has Jesus take twelve men with him, moving more deeply into the journey of faith, walking towards Jerusalem. He points himself towards Jerusalem, which symbolises for him 'the meaning of his life'. It shows the purpose of his life, which is doing the father's will. In doing that, he experiences within himself the freedom the Good News promises.

So, Jesus invites his brothers to walk with him, mistakes and all. In other words, you have to enter into the experience and then you will know who God is for you. So much of theology is trying to prove who God is; the important question to answer is who God is for you and then you know, in effect, who God is. And that is Mark's wisdom.

Many years ago, my friend Cathy went to one of her first prayer meetings with her friend Eileen. While she was there, she shared something that she had discovered in prayer about the love of God. After she had shared, a Jesuit priest who was there, and obviously feeling a bit threatened by what she said, stood up. He looked at her and, in quite an aggressive tone, said to her, 'Where do you get your theology from?' Cathy was not at all overwhelmed by this and looked back at him and said, 'From my experience of God. Where do you get yours from?' She had discovered who God was for her. She has continued to do that down the years, and I have come to realise that there is nothing that can shake that sort of knowledge and that is what Mark wants us to discover.

Mark does have Jesus proclaim the glory of God by miracles, signs and wonders, but you will find that in every miracle story there is a counter to that story, a pulling in the other direction. Mark invites you think of the cost involved in walking the Jesus way. Mark wants to show us that Jesus is the unique Son of God but only in terms of the suffering servant. We will understand who God is for us when we see the crucified Lord. We will know then that God is the eternal giver. That eternal giving of God is dramatised and personalised in the crucified Jesus. When we see Jesus on the cross, we see him in his moment of loneliness but, ironically, his moment of Lordship.

At the beginning of the Gospel, Jesus is caught up with the crowds all around him but as the Gospel progresses you find him moving out of the crowds to fewer and fewer people so fewer can understand him. Until finally at the foot of the cross there is no one who is able to confess that 'Jesus is Lord' except, ironically, a pagan centurion. One person in Jesus' moment of absolute loneliness is free to see that Jesus is Lord. When he was in the crowd working miracles, they were all cheering him. When he was on the cross, only the Centurion said this was truly the Son of God and yet that is the climax of the gospel, at the very end.

The very first words that come out of the mouth of Jesus are 'Repent and believe the good news'. Some while back I wrote a book on the word, metanoia, which we translate as the loaded word 'repent', seeing it as having something to do with sin and the need for forgiveness. It comes from two Greek words: Meta, meaning above; and Nous, meaning mind. Metanoia invites us to move beyond our default setting, into a much broader understanding where we buy into a bigger picture that Jesus calls the kingdom of God. This kingdom living means that we move beyond our inclinations for self-interest and self-protection which so frequently dog us. This results in bitterness, negativity, and lack of empathy inside us which then affects the world around us.

My mum grew up in inner city Liverpool. When the bombs fell

and much of the city was crushed and broken mum and her family found themselves homeless for a short while. They went to live with my grandmother's sister until they found themselves a new house to rent not to far from their ruined one. In the next street to them, lived three sisters. They were Catholics and would go to Mass each week. Two of them were very gentle loving souls who were completely dominated by the third sister. Mary was a bitter, angry woman who seemed to fall out with everyone, even my lovely, gentle, saint of a grandmother. For her sisters' sake, my mum always kept in touch, and each Christmas day the three of them would come for tea. The tension would rise as Mary, in her red velvet dress, would sit at the table and spit out venom and gossip about the neighbours, and other parishioners. Her beady eyes would weigh up everything on the table and in a very genteel voice she would criticise what she saw. As a child I was frightened by her but now I wonder what it was that led her to be the way she was. Whatever had hurt her in her life, her faith did not seem to move her beyond it. When she died, there were just five people at her funeral - her two sisters, my aunty Maureen, mum and myself. Bitterness, negativity, and lack of empathy breeds its own reward

Metanoia invites us to bring openness and warmth to every situation we face, even those which are negative. Moreover, metanoia stands in contrast to paranoia. Ronald Rolheiser says, 'In essence, metanoia is 'non-paranoia', so that Jesus' opening words in the Synoptic Gospels might be better rendered: Be un-paranoid and believe that it is good news. Live in trust!'

That is how Jesus lived and that is what Mark presents to us as he has Jesus walk towards Calvary. Jesus hangs on the cross as a visual image of what it means to have surrendered to metanoia. On the cross, Jesus is exposed and defenceless. He has no need to protect himself. His arms are open wide to embrace every man and woman. That, of course, is the opposite to the defended, closed, suspicious stance of paranoia. Metanoia is always about the bigger heart, the wider mind which never closes doors.

Julia Broderick was a dramatic little woman from Manchester. She was tiny in stature with enormous blue eyes that looked out on the world without guile. Julia had married the love of her life, Tom, just before the second world war. Tom was unable to fight for medical reasons. His one sadness was that he and Julia were unable to have children. This led the two of them to be totally wrapped up in each other. They lived in a small rented terraced house and I could feel the love and contentment whenever we visited them. They were friends of my grandmother despite being much younger than her. In my teenage years, I thought of them as being a bit strange, slightly naïve and innocent. Now with the wisdom of years, I have realised that in fact they were just totally unprotected. They had nothing to defend and so were lovely, open, warm people who just exuded love wherever they went. Right at the heart of their lives was faith. God mattered to them more than anything else. They prayed together each day. They went to Mass as often as they could. They shared what they had with those less fortunate. As I look back now, I understand that their life of faith was what made them wonderfully open, and loving and I also know that metanoia had happened, and was always happening, within them both. When her Tom died, Julia was devastated but carried on for a few more years. She was about to go to Lourdes when she rang my mum and thanked her for all the years of friendship. When she arrived in Lourdes, she took ill, and died and was buried there. The phone call was her last goodbye, but her legacy lives on in the hearts and minds of those who knew her. Her legacy? It was love, openness, warmth and kindness!

Mark's Jesus, in the message he proclaims in both word and action, invites us to metanoia, to move towards and stay within our bigger minds and bigger hearts, so that in the face of suffering, pain, and even the cross, we can remain open and all embracing.

FIVE

THE JESUS EXPERIENCE

One of the freest people I have ever met is Edwina Gately. On her web site it says, 'Edwina is a poet, theologian, artist, writer, and lay minister. She is a single mum and has been described as a modern-day mystic and prophet.' Edwina came to Southport to speak at one of our conferences several years ago. She was a great communicator but, as she shared her stories about her life's experience, I realised that I was in the presence of someone very special. She oozed the essence of humanity with her compassion and her understanding. Full of humour and sensitivity, she had no time for the trammels of life and simply responded to where she felt God was leading her; and God has definitely led her. From her early life in Lancaster, she found herself teaching in Africa. She started the Volunteer Missionary Movement which is still a force today. She was then led into the Sahara Desert where she spent time reflecting and praying. She is the friend and minister to street people and women in prostitution. Her stories are colourful and vibrant, not least because of the descriptive, and sometimes ripe, language she uses! She has a very simple and profound message that God is with us and particularly to be found in those who are in need.

As I spent time with her, I found myself both fascinated and challenged by her freedom. I think, too, that I became aware that her freedom to listen to God and to respond to God had cost her a great deal. Undoubtedly, Edwina has suffered in her following of the promptings of the Spirit. She has been misunderstood and, at times, scapegoated by others who do not quite understand. Still, she ploughs on, relentless in her desire to respond to the Gospel.

In the last chapter we reflected on the Christ that Mark presents to us, a very human Christ who comes to his glory through the way of the cross. He is a man who has no time for the social niceties of his day, so much so that his friends and his family thought he was crazy and wanted to lock him up. In this chapter I want to reflect on the suffering Christ, which is key to understanding the man Mark presents to us and the key and central teaching on the kingdom which helps us to understand the Jesus that Mark communicates.

There are two movements in Mark's Gospel. The first one builds up to chapter 8:29 where Peter says almost tentatively, 'You are the Christ.' The whole of these chapters are revealing to us who this Jesus is. The second movement begins from it and goes to the end of the Gospel and it is all about the mystery of the suffering Christ.

Mark is challenging us to recognise the divine in the ordinariness of human life and in the mess that most of us live in. He is showing us how often we are unable to perceive the divine in the world, and much of his Gospel is trying to enable us to see more clearly the presence of God in everything. We are invited to see it particularly in the cross, in ugliness and weakness and failure; indeed in much of what we call humanity.

About thirty years ago I went into a bad depression and ended up having a lot of therapy. I felt useless and wondered whether I should stay a priest because everything about priesthood frightened me. Surprisingly, it was also the time when I have felt God most closely, particularly in the people who listened to me and helped me to understand myself.

When you have learnt to recognise God, you have entered into the Jesus experience, an experience which is essentially about relationship, a relationship that Jesus had to his father. It is in no way understandable, even to common sense. It is in no way understandable in a logical way. This is theological. It is God's logic, which is an upside-down logic as far as the world is concerned. Only the Spirit of God can help us to understand that. Only walking the journey that Jesus walked can help us to understand it. With that as an overall view, we have the first chapter of Mark.

It begins, 'The beginning of the good news about Jesus Christ, the Son of God.' Right at the beginning of the Gospel, Mark makes his affirmation about the Lord Jesus. As soon as he says Jesus Christ, Mark is already affirming something of his belief in him. He does not begin with the birth narrative of Jesus because he wants us to know that the story begins much further back than that. It begins in the mind and heart of God and has existed for all eternity. There has never been a moment when God has not wanted to redeem the world in Christ.

We all know that Christ is not his last name; Christ is his title.

It means the anointed one or the Messiah. Mark is reminding the reader that he has made the decision to believe that Jesus is the anointed one who is revealing to us the face of God. We are told that he is the Son of God, and immediately we are challenged to ask, what does it mean for us to say that Jesus is the Son of God?

Mark has made a decision to believe in this truth. It is a very Jewish affirmation. The idea of the Messiah comes out of Judaism. Throughout the first testament there is a growing awareness that God was coming to save humanity. That awareness rose to a point where the Jewish nation waited desperately for this coming Messiah. There was an expectancy among the Jews that the Messiah would reveal to them who God is in space and time. This intervention of God was called the day of the Lord.

Some of the Jews expected a political Messiah, someone who would make them a great nation and free them from the Roman Occupation. It was true that they were to become a great nation, but it was spiritual greatness they were destined for and that greatness was far beyond their understanding.

Mark was obviously being drawn into understanding Hebrew spirituality. Mark knows the truth of the Shema, the Deuteronomic law. It is all about faithful love. It is about God's love for us and our love for God and for God's people. It is an understanding that Jesus is the fulfillment of everything that Israel hoped for. What happens to Mark somehow has to happen to us. We cannot enter into the second Testament experience unless we understand our Jewish roots. If that is true, and I believe it is, then it becomes very difficult to understand why so much of Christian history has been anti-Semitic. As Richard Rohr says; to understand Jesus we have to think like a Jew, taste like a Jew, have the heart of a Jew, the lungs of a Jew. We have got to explore Judaism to understand Jesus. If we do not have an experience of the First Testament, then we lose so much of the meaning of Jesus. To understand what the people of Israel suffered and what they hoped for is crucial in understanding the Gospel. Although Mark is not Jewish, he seems to know how a Jew thinks. That is why he is able to make the affirmation that Jesus is the Christ.

The Jews have, at best, a hazy concept of an afterlife. That is so difficult for us as Christians to understand. As I have often said, we have made religion what we do to get into another world, which makes it, by implication, not take this world seriously. Jesus was a Jew and he knew how to live life and to enjoy family. He made it obvious that life was worth living. He went to parties and weddings and meals. He was obviously gregarious and full of humour – who would have invited him if he was a lugubrious misery!

When we learn that God believes in us and in this world and in the stuff of humanity, then we can believe in ourselves. It is a sad fact that much of Church history has said that God does not believe in us as we are, that we have to change to get into another world. It just illustrates what happens when we lose our Jewish roots. When we cut off our Jewish roots, we do not understand ourselves or God. One of the major problems with the renewal of the Church is that we do not know our own truths. When we get in touch with that Hebrew tradition, it will free us, so we can understand what life is about and what God is about.

Religion is to enable people to live a full life and that involves taking on the reality of suffering and living it. Faith is not a stance or position you adopt to get into another world. You do not get in touch with God just to get brownie points to get into heaven. That is not the meaning of our relationship. It is a prostitution of it. The reason we come to know God is simply that God is love and God is for us. We are called simply to be human and alive, to be the sons of God and daughters of the Lord.

When I was a student for the priesthood, I met a man called David. During the summer vacation, students were encouraged to take on some pastoral work and I arranged a placement at Hettinga House. Hettinga was a branch of Jospice, an organisation set up by Fr Francis O'Leary to care for those who are terminally ill. David lived in Hettinga House with a life limiting illness. He was paraplegic and he had to have everything done for him even down to evacuating his bowels. David was full of good humour, sometimes very dark humour, but funny, nonetheless. He laughed his way through life even when the most intimate things were being done to him.

One day I was showering him, and we were chatting away and laughing as per usual. I was suddenly and acutely aware of his lack of physical dignity and I stopped laughing. I asked him how he could stand people doing all the things that they had to do for him. I will never forget his answer. He told me that God had created him as he was. He knew that he was loved, and nothing could ever take that away from him not even the reality of his disabilities. That day, I saw immense dignity that could not be shattered by what I thought was the worst indignity possible. David knew that he was a child of God.

As Mark continues to share the good news of Christ, he writes, 'The time has come; the Kingdom of God is at hand, turn around and believe the good news.' Somehow all the evangelists saw Jesus' teaching summed up in that sentence, and the amazing thing is that to most of us it seems so innocuous. And that tells us how far we have come from the contemporary situation that Jesus was trying to preach to, and why we do not really deal with the right issues.

I am sure in my own formation the teaching on the kingdom of God was hardly mentioned. A typical Catholic thinks that the hallmark of being Catholic is going to Mass on Sunday. In all of Jesus' teaching we do not even see that alluded to and we yet can spend so much trying to convince people that the be all and end-all of Christian life is going to Mass on Sunday.

Jesus proclaims the Kingdom of God. He says something new is happening. In fact, it has always been happening but now I am here to personalise it for you. I am here to let it happen in my body, in my experience, so you can know it can happen in you.

Jesus knew that we were incarnate beings and we need

sacraments and symbols. We cannot act in a totally abstract way. We have to see it personified, to let it happen in us. We have to be in a relationship with the person for whom it has happened and in whom it has happened, before it can happen in us.

People change in the context of relationships. We so often move the gospel out of the relational context back into the cerebral, head context. When we moved the verbal level and the ideological level to the centre of the stage, we lost much of our power to really transform lives and to change hearts. So, Jesus, the incarnate God, had to be relatable to.

The concept of the kingdom is very difficult to put words on. I often think that Jesus himself could not describe the kingdom, which is why he said over and over the kingdom of God is like... However, there are words which imply something of the kingdom - relationship, belief, trusting, hope. It is a way of seeing yourself. It is a way of dying and it is a way of living. Its major tenet is that God is father, in the way that the Jewish myth understood fatherhood. That is the essence of the new and absolutely clear teaching of Jesus - that God is father. I wonder how many of us really understand that truth?

I am well aware, of course, that our own experience of fatherhood can make that difficult, but try and understand the Jewish myth and move beyond your own experience to understand more fully. No religion had ever understood the warm and protective nature of God like Jesus did. Jesus took his Jewish understanding of ownership and inheritance and made it even more. Jesus did not just sit and give teaching on the father. He let it happen within him. In other words, in his obedience, trust and hope in his father's protection, he allowed God to guide his whole life. He let what he discerned to be the will of the father lead him to unbelievable ends. He let it lead him to crucifixion. The important thing was to be true to God; to be faithful to God with the trust and hope that God would raise him up. That is why the resurrection becomes the great act of faithfulness of God. It is not a proof that Jesus is God.

The only way that anyone comes to believe that Jesus is Lord and believe in the divinity of Jesus Christ, is by opening up to grace. It means a relationship to God in which we allow God to take over our hearts, in which we allow ourselves to lose control. It is an invitation to let go and surrender ourselves. Faith is a gift. It is a gift from God. It is simply a matter of wanting that gift, desiring to be in the relationship. That relationship, in Jesus' language, is the kingdom of God.

I remember being terribly moved watching the film version of Corrie Ten Boom's life. She found herself in the Dutch resistance movement and was eventually sent to Ravensbruck concentration camp. There is a scene in the film where Corrie's number is called out during the roll call. She is convinced that it means certain death because it has in every other similar situation. As she leaves the ranks of women, one who has been a thorn in her side, and yet at times helpful to her and her sister Betsie, catches hold of her hand. She looks at Corrie and with every fibre of her being says, 'Corrie, I want him'. With tears tripping down her face

Corrie responds saying, 'Ask him.' That is all it takes. Get in touch with your desire for God. Get in touch with your need for God and ask. God will always respond.

Then Mark writes, 'The time has come.' This is it. Everything we need to be a fully alive human being is here. We do not have to search any more. There is nothing else to come that is going to complete the world or help us understand who we are. In Jesus, the fullness of time has come. Mark is almost pleading with us to realise what has been given and what is available to us. We have been given everything we need if we will accept and believe in the kingdom of God. God is totally available to us. God is not withholding Godself. God is available to us. God is a perfectly open door. The door that never closes.

There is nothing to withhold us from God's grace and God's light and God's perfect acceptance. The only thing that can do that is our lack of faith. The way this is spoken about in the Gospels is in terms of our own inability to believe. To believe in the kingdom, to believe in God's love, is not simply a head belief; that Jesus is the ontological Son of God. To believe in the Jesus experience and to allow him to draw us into his relationship with the father, moves faith out of the head into the whole person. So, faith is not simply an intellectual response, it is a personal response, it is a decision. Love is a decision. Relationship is a decision. Salvation is a decision. Do we want to be liberated by his love?

The announcement of the good news is that God loves us, and we do not have to play games, or to try to earn that love. Indeed, once we have to play games for love it does not liberate, it ensnares. Only grace frees. Only love that is not worked for, that is not manipulated, transforms.

The next phrase is repent. Turnaround. You have to make that decision. The Greek word is metanoia, a key word in understanding the Gospel. It is decision language. We have got to turn round from what the world sees as reality and believe in the Lord's reality, which is the Kingdom of God.

This Kingdom then frees us to live in the kingdom of this earth. It puts us back into the world in a free way, knowing that we cannot be controlled by the systems and structures of this world. It frees us so that we can plunge into the depths of the world because the world no longer has any hold over us. It means we can freely stand against injustice and lack of love because we are not dependent on what others are dependent on. When the world sees liberated, free people, then it is going to believe. When it sees people who are not reliant on market forces or political systems of the day, it is going to ask the question, 'What do you have? How can you live this way?' Until the concept of the Kingdom is clearly within, we cannot understand the rest of the gospel and the call Mark gives to walk the Jesus way of suffering to find life.

I often see the reality of the kingdom in those who come to our choir. It is for those living with a dementia and their carers. It is extraordinary to see how music affects those who have dementia. One old lady, Joyce, used to come from a local home. She was in a wheelchair with her head bent over staring at the floor. The only words she ever used were swear words until the music started and then Joyce would come to life. I also sensed the presence of God in those who brought her and catered for her every need.

As I look into the faces of Betty and Bill, a husband and wife, or Mary and her children, or Sue and her mum Betty, I see the willingness to go that extra mile and be the sign of love that is the kingdom. Somehow they have realised, through necessity maybe, what is really important in life - love, forgiveness and caring. Just recently I was talking to Harry who was heartbroken because Joan, on a few occasions, had failed to recognise him. I asked him what that felt like. He said it tore him apart inside, but he said, 'Thank God I know who she is, and I can still give her the love that she needs.' The kingdom is indeed in our midst as people live out their lives in extraordinary service and love of one another.

Immediately after his proclaiming of the Kingdom of God, Jesus calls his first four disciples into it. It is as though Jesus is saying 'Come into relationship with me and something is going to happen between us that is so good, that is so real and that will be so attractive, that others are going to be caught by it and want to experience it. So, you see, Jesus did not proclaim an abstract gospel.

When you understand what you are called to, then you are prepared to give your life for that great and glorious Gospel, but it is costly. It costs our very lives and so, after all the rhetoric about the Kingdom, Jesus begins to teach about the suffering way of the cross.

Mark tells us that Jesus and the disciples left for the village around Caesarea Philippi. And on the way he put this question to his disciples, 'Who do people say that I am.' Then he challenges them with that question which has haunted me down the years, 'And you, who do you say I am?' Peter, the spokesman for the first community stands up and says very simply, 'You are the Christ'. It is just as if the first 8 chapters have led the first community to this tentative place of faith. That is the way Mark hopes to have taken us. If we follow these 8 chapters and learn the lesson of trusting and faith and presence then maybe we too can believe that this is the Christ. Ironically, straight after, he gave strict instructions not tell anyone.

I learnt the lesson of trusting faith from my Nana who was born in 1892, the eldest of three daughters in an Irish immigrant family. At some point, my great grandparents left Ireland and the story goes that they met each other on the boat to Liverpool. They were on their way to America but ran out of money when they arrived in Liverpool. They got married and stayed there in Bootle, a small town near Liverpool. My great grandfather, James Hughes, was a docker who got work when he could. Life was hard and they lived from hand to mouth in the courts of Bootle just scraping the rent together each week and eating when they could. The courts were squares of back to back houses with a shared toilet in the middle. They were nearly always slums, with several families living in one house, sometimes just a room for each family. Right at the centre of Nana's family's life was their faith, and Nana grew up praying every day and learning how to trust the goodness of God despite the tough circumstance of her life. She lived with us when I was a child, an elderly sick woman, but her faith shone from her eyes. This was particularly true as she held me in her arms when my dad was drunk and would whisper to me that everything would be alright because God loved us. She would often tell me that God had never let her down and there was no need to be afraid. Trusting and faithful even in the face of adversity.

Mark says that Jesus now heads for Jerusalem; three times he will accept his role as the suffering servant, three times he will be misunderstood and three times he will try to teach the disciples about the mystery of life coming through death. So immediately after Peter's confession, Mark has Jesus begin to teach that the son of man was destined to suffer. Life comes through death. However, the disciples are expecting a total resurrection community. With Jesus, they thought everything would be wonderful. That is not the case. It all comes through suffering. Peter cannot accept that suffering is God's way. Jesus has to rebuke him in the hardest terms. We then find Jesus encouraging Christians to take up the cross, to walk his way and Mark begins to unpack what it means for Jesus to be Isaiah's suffering servant and what it will mean for us.

SIX

SUFFERING FOR THE SAKE OF THE WORLD

I often find myself privileged to listen to people's stories. Just recently a woman called Norah came to see me. Norah lives many miles from me but her friend who I see regularly had asked if she could come. She was a lovely person, who almost immediately she sat down began to tell her story. It was as though the pain of years burst forth like a dam that had been breached.

Born illegitimate, her early life was difficult as her mother tried to make ends meet in a small village in Wales where everybody knew everybody else's business. It was the 1940's and they were shunned by many of their good, Christian neighbours. Her early years at school were marked by bullying. She described how she had cried on her first communion day, because a boy had poured ink over her. It was because she did not have a dad and the language he used was choice as he laughed and called her names.

When she was nine her mother married and Norah's step father resented the child who was not his own. While her mother tried to protect her, the animosity grew as did the violence meted out to both Norah and her mother. When she was fifteen, Norah's mother died suddenly, and she was thrown out of the house and had to make her own way in the world. Alone and friendless she had to find herself a job and somewhere to live. Life was hard and continued to be so. She described the breakdown of her two marriages, the death of her daughter at the age of twenty from drugs. She talked of her son's mental health issues and the loneliness of her life. The pain that she shared was almost tangible. At some point on her journey she had encountered God and began to see the pain in her life as the cross. That helped her to cope a little better than she might have done otherwise. While living in the midst of all this brokenness she qualified as a Psychiatric nurse. It was because she knew that she understood the mental pain that can afflict so many people and she wanted to help others. She started to work in her spare time with homeless young people, taking some into her home to give them a chance. That too was the cross in her life as she took on the pain of others and walked alongside them.

I suppose many of us experience things in our lives that we call the cross. It may be illness or bereavement or some sort of difficulty that we have to cope with and in many ways, it can be a comfort to think of it as the cross. Having said that there is a very real sense in which Mark in his gospel sees suffering as something much wider and bigger than only the pain and difficulty that we as individuals have to face in life, although that is very much part of it and I would like first of all to reflect on that. Then I would like to think about the wider implication of suffering for the sake of the Gospel. Undoubtedly Mark has the cross stand at the centre of his Gospel demanding our attention. It is right at the centre of our faith. I sometimes wonder why? Why should a crucified man be the icon of redemption and what is he about for those of us who say we follow him?

I think it is fair to say that for all of us life contains suffering. It is impossible to avoid it. I think what the cross says to us is that suffering is not a waste of time, that it has a redemptive purpose, that it can bring life. Learning to take up the cross and surrender our lives is an invitation to be at peace with what life throws at us without bitterness or rancour. Is that not the way in which Jesus counteracts his suffering, by absorbing it into himself and not allowing it to make him bitter? We are to do the same with our own pain. Try not to run away from it, but discover what it means. The hardest times in my life have also been the most life giving as I have tried to discover what my pain was telling me. Do not try and protect yourself from hurt. Do not put up the barriers against love, which always hurts at some point.

Walking in the footsteps of Jesus as he carries his cross is an invitation to accept that death is part of life. We have in some senses to die to ourselves. It is an invitation to die to our anger, our bitterness, our hurts, our hatred. I have met too many people who are held bound by their inner condition and who cling on to what their pain is rather than letting it go. I have also met some extraordinary people like Norah in whom there was no trace of bitterness or anger as she shared her story. To see the cross as central to faith is about dying to self. Ronald Rolheiser, the Canadian oblate, says, 'Maturity and Christian discipleship are about perennially naming our deaths, claiming our births, mourning our losses, letting go of what's died, and receiving new spirit for the new life that we are now living.' Every year we celebrate ritually the paschal mystery. It is meant to be *our* story as well as the age-old story of Jesus. His story is our story and our story is his story.

Recognising the power of the cross is an invitation to live life in hope. It is to know that much of life contains disappointment but that for those who follow Jesus, waiting and longing for the bigger picture is part of the story. My friend Mary campaigns for justice for the Palestinians. She visits the country regularly and has witnessed first- hand the injustice and the brokenness. She refuses to be bitter and angry about the situation that the Palestinians find themselves in and admits that waiting for the big picture to be fulfilled is part of the story. She knows that she may never see it and it is frustrating for her, but she waits in joyful hope. As Rolheiser says, 'So much of life and discipleship is about waiting, waiting in frustration, inside injustice, inside pain, in longing, battling bitterness, as we wait for something or someone to come and change our situation.'

I read recently that James Martin the Jesuit author says that to carry our cross is to be open to surprises. I remember the very powerful book by Gerard Hughes, *The God of Surprises*, in which he tries to share the surprising presence of God in our lives. Who knows what, or whom, we will encounter on the journey? Did Jesus expect the gift of Simon of Cyrene? Or his followers the gift of Joseph of Arimathea? Glimpses of resurrection are often ours if we have eyes to see and are open to the God of surprises. To take up our cross and surrender our lives means recognising that God is bigger and more than we can ever imagine. It is about living in trusting hope, that, in the words of Julian of Norwich,

'All will be well, and all manner of things will be well.' I might not see it or experience it now, but God is always more. Rolheiser again comments, 'It is only possible to accept our cross, to live in trust, and to not grow bitter inside pain if we believe in possibilities beyond what we can imagine; namely, if we believe in the Resurrection. We can take up our cross when we begin to believe in the Resurrection.'

I think as well as the cross that we bear in our personal life, the cross is always an invitation to enter into the pain of the world. It is a reminder to us that following the Gospel way will involve suffering. We cannot avoid it. We will be rejected and treated as though we were crazy and unable to understand the real world. Mark has Jesus reflect on what it means to be a disciple after Peter's declaration of faith, and it is a hard message to take. The son of man was destined to suffer. If you are going to say that Jesus is the Christ and walk in his way, then you will need to discover that real life only comes through suffering. To follow Jesus is to take on the pain of others and somehow, in taking on that pain, transform it into life.

This is a real challenge not to run away from the pain of the world but to enter into it. The only way to enter into life is to enter it through death. We have to let ourselves be vulnerable. We have to allow ourselves to be weak. We have to encounter life and be touched and broken by it. If we do not, then Christianity remains beautiful poetry or deep philosophy. That is the example of Jesus. It cost to heal the sick emotionally and physically. It cost Jesus not to give in to his own needs and desires. It cost him to face his own pain and hurt but he did it so we would know the truth that from each death comes life.

When we take up the cross, we become witnesses to the Jesus way. That way is all about love and compassion. I was trying to reflect the other day on the word compassion. What is compassion? What is love? At the core of the Gospel is a God who has compassion for the world. This wonderful gift that we live in was created out of infinite love. We were created out of that same love. The depth of God's love means that God suffers with those who are broken and in pain. God is moved in the depths of God's being so much so that God chose to live in the midst of this messy world. So this compassionate merciful God became flesh in Jesus so that we could see in a human person the face of God and have an encounter with the compassion of God who in Jesus frees us from our fear and the mess that is all around us and turns us around to see that life is wonderful because of the gift of God. It is that same compassion that fills our hearts by the gift of the Spirit. To walk the Jesus way is to allow that compassion to flow from us into the world.

One of the most compassionate people I know is a priest called Richard McKay. I have met him on several occasions and have marvelled at his capacity to walk alongside refugees and displaced people. In 1978, he moved from working in Taunton in Somerset to Knowle West in Bristol, a very run-down poor community with very high inter-generational unemployment and over-crowded housing. It was a broken community that had no hope! Richard admits that he struggled to adapt to this completely different community. At that time, he heard about Oscar Romero living and working in El Salvador in Central America. Richard was captivated by Romero and his struggle. Romero became the Archbishop of El Salvador and was immediately faced with the huge problems his people had to endure. They were poor and repressed by the country's dictatorship, often having to deal with government violence and murder.

All of this led to a change in Romero's life. He was converted to a life of Christ-like courage and became the voice of the poor. He would not be silenced, even when his life was threatened and the Church's radio station that broadcast his sermons every Sunday was blown up. On the 24th March 1980, while celebrating Mass in a convent chapel, a government assassin shot him dead.

Richard was in the kitchen of the presbytery in Knowle West having breakfast when he heard the news. He says at that moment he knew that God had placed a call on his life. He was to spend his life sharing with, and living for, the poor. He says, 'As a priest, a shepherd of God's people, Oscar Romero has inspired me and changed the course of my life and my understanding of the message of Jesus. I see in him, this Shepherd of the poor and Prophet of Justice, this Voice of the voiceless, the person of Jesus, risen and alive today'.

Since then Richard has done just that with immense compassion. His parish in Bristol is a haven of welcome for people of all sorts of persuasions and the community walk alongside so called 'failed' asylum seekers, and those seeking asylum, refugees, sex workers and ex- prisoners to name just a few groups.

To walk the Jesus way means to see every individual as a unique creation of God, whoever they may be. It is to have our hearts torn apart because of the pain of the world and it is to stand on the side of those most rejected by society, the asylum seeker, the refugee, the outcast, the aids sufferer and those who live on the edges of society. This will inevitably lead to clashes and disagreements, because to be on the side of the little one is to press the buttons of those who are controlled by their ego and live terrified of losing what little power they think they have. That conflict, and the suffering and rejection that can come from it, is the cross.

There is talk of building a hostel for the homeless in our area. I went along to the residents meeting. There were about one hundred people there. I could count on one hand those who were in favour of the hostel being opened. There was a lot of anger and the typical 'not in my back yard' comments. I spoke a couple of times and was struck by the animosity with which my interjections were greeted. The morning after the meeting, I met one of my neighbours, who I am on speaking terms with. I said, 'Good morning' and she deliberately turned her head and looked the other way. To stand for the Gospel always involves the cross.

When we begin to allow the Gospel values of forgiveness, peace, understanding and acceptance to permeate our lives and influence how we both live and react to others, then it will bring us into conflict. It is inevitable because it holds a mirror up to the standards and lives of others. I love this quotation that I came across recently from Tullian Tchividjian, who is an American clergyman. He wrote, 'The gospel alone liberates you to live a life of scandalous generosity, unrestrained sacrifice, uncommon valour, and unbounded courage.' When we carry the cross of the pain and tragedy of the world, we need to be generous, sacrificial and strong. I think that is particularly true when we begin to recognise how important the values of simplicity and just living are. The questioning of the economic systems that control society and allow some to starve while others live on the backs of the poor will inevitably become part of life. It is very interesting to see the response of the authorities against the climate control protestors in London as I write this chapter. It seems to be all about power and maintaining the systems that surround us.

To take up the cross is an invitation to enter into the pain of the world, to feel the pain of those struggling for justice and experiencing persecution and to do what we can to alleviate those realities. To take up the cross is to feel the pain of those whose dignity is eroded by unjust government policies here in our own country. It is to try and walk with those who have to resort to food banks and who live with the threat of homelessness. To take up the cross is to stand alongside those who suffer from discrimination of any form, entering into the needs of others and helping others find life in the death that they experience. It is to experience suffering and rejection because of our willingness to stand for Gospel truth and to absorb those things and return them in love and compassion. The scorn of, and the dismissal from others, for the sake of the Gospel, is the cross.

Dietrich Bonhoeffer was a lecturer in theology at the University of Berlin in Germany in the 1930's. The German Christians were divided over Hitler. One group was on Hitler's side. They wanted what they called a 'pure' German nation. They formed an official German church, which supported Hitler's view and banned Jews from holding official positions in the Church. Bonhoeffer was among those who could not go along with Hitler's anti-Jewish, German vision. Along with others, he set up an underground church. This group explicitly refused to sell out to Hitler's Third Reich vision. It was a dangerous thing to do and of course it was discovered. So, in 1937 Bonhoeffer was sacked from his university job and he left Germany and went to live in London.

Two years later Bonhoeffer was faced with a choice. He was offered one of the most prestigious theology appointments in the world. This involved taking up a lectureship at the Union Seminary in New York or returning to Germany to lead an illegal, underground seminary for the churches who refuse to go along with Hitler's world view. Bonhoeffer was a man of deep integrity and he decided that his faith meant nothing if he took the easy option and went to New York. He went home to Germany where he was horrified at Hitler's evil message and the state of his country. He had always been a pacifist but faced with this he abandoned his commitment to non-violence and got involved in a plot to assassinate Hitler. The plot failed and, in 1943, Bonhoeffer was arrested. While was in prison he led worship services for his fellow prisoners, until the fateful day 9th April 1945 when he was executed by the Nazis. What distressed Bonhoeffer more than anything else was the way so many Christians could adopt

Hitler's evil vision. He could never understand how people who professed to be Christians could so betray Christ and his Gospel. How could they pray in a church while supporting such an evil regime? How could they not stand for those who were being persecuted by that regime? How could they compromise on love, the core value of the Gospel, to save themselves? It convinced Bonhoeffer that religion, in and of itself, was worthless. For him it did not matter how much a person purported to believe in Jesus. It was not important how many times each day they prayed, how devoutly and sincerely they sang hymns on Sundays. In the end the measure of faith in Jesus is not how we are in the church but how we are in our ordinary lives. In the end the acid test of our faith is to live in the world as a man or woman who is for others whatever the cost, however difficult that may make our own lives.

Mark's Jesus does not offer us an easy life when he invites us to take up the cross and become, like him, the suffering servant. It demands metanoia within us, it demands transformation within us. Everything that we are told by the media that is necessary for a happy and fulfilled life, material wealth, sexual prowess, a strong egocentric push for life fades into insignificance in the shadow of the call to carry the cross. In fact, the opposite becomes true, as we discover that human fulfilment does not lie in possessions, power or prestige but in the laying down of those things. It seems to me as I travel and look around the Christian world that very few people are prepared to live in this way.

My own Catholic tradition, which I love, is besmirched with sexual scandal and with a neo-conservatism amongst younger clergy. This, along with other issues, is causing people to walk away in their droves. I see a huge amount of energy wasted on ritual and getting ritual right. I am, sadly, aware that there is a need for many to be doctrinally correct and pure, and that orthodoxy is of immense importance to a huge part of the Church, but I do not see too many people who carry the cross and who live as the suffering servant. We are living in a culture where people are desperate for others to walk with them in their need and as Church all we seem to be anxious about is not losing 'my mass'. How can that be the Gospel of Jesus? This Jesus who says 'take up your cross and follow me' .

Ronnie was a fantastic man whom I knew all of my life until his untimely death at a relatively young age. He was born and bred in Liverpool and became a Catholic in his twenties when he married the love of his life, Joan. He was a man who was concerned with people and with the Gospel. He would help anyone particularly those who were poor or widowed. I was walking through town with him one day when he met a man shivering with cold. Ronnie immediately took his coat off and gave it to the man and then went and got him some food and a hot drink. Afterwards I asked him what impelled him to do that and he said in his broad scouse accent, 'It's what I'm here for mate.' He was part of the St Vincent de Paul society in his parish and would often find himself in trouble with others in the group as he refused to check out anyone's credentials before giving help. He simply responded to a cry for help. To take up the cross is to value people more than anything else in life and to let love and compassion flow.

So, the invitation Mark's Jesus gives us is to take up the cross. There will be conflict for those who follow the Jesus way and there will be suffering, there will be the cross. Beware of anyone who preaches resurrection without the cross. Thank God faith tells us that taking up the cross is not the whole story. If it was, we would die, we could not cope. If we take up the cross, with all that means, then somehow our suffering and the suffering of the world will be transformed into glory just as Jesus' was. Somehow each and every death we inevitably go through will give way to life. That is the promise of Jesus, that we will be filled with joy and life that nothing and no-one can take away from us not just in the future but in the here and now.

So, to the challenge! Are we prepared to go the extra mile for those who have no-one to be there for them and who at times need a listening ear? Are we known for the level of compassion in our parish communities? Are our communities' places of healing love for those who are at the end of their tether? What about those who exhibit unreasonable behaviour and live on the edges? How do we respond? It is not always easy to walk alongside others. It can be very costly as we have to take the risk to let go of ingrained attitudes and prejudices and take up the call to be compassionate. It is a long hard slog to take the risk to be with the poor and the needy, who, because of their pain, can often be ungrateful. Sometimes we are challenged to let go of the neat little religious package we have created for ourselves and to listen to the promptings of the Spirit in order to let compassion flow like a river. I guess to take up the cross demands that we call on the power of God to fill us and empower us and God always answers that prayer.

SEVEN

THE INCLUSIVITY OF GOD

I was coming from the shops just recently and noticed one of our volunteers chatting with a young girl on our car park. Maureen left her, and went into the meeting she was due at, and the girl began to wander away. I noticed she was crying, so I caught up with her. She told me that her name was Rachel and that she had only just moved into the area. Then the floodgates opened as she told me that this was meant to be a new start for her, but her life was falling apart. She had spent some time in a psychiatric unit after trying to take her own life. This was as a result of abuse at the hands of her father who was now serving a long prison sentence. Her family wanted nothing to do with her because they blamed her for her father's incarceration.

She said that she had been in the unit for a couple of years, so I guessed she was pretty fragile if she needed that much care. Now that she was supposedly well, she had been let out. It seemed that there was little aftercare other than psychiatric appointment in three months time. She was unable to get benefits and there were no crisis loans available. She had a roof over her head thanks to an old friend. We managed to get some food for her, and I went with her to where she lived and paid her friend some rent. While we were on the way, Rachel said something to me that pulled at my heartstrings. She said that she just wanted somewhere to belong and to feel safe. I guess that is true for most human beings.

We want to be safe and we want to belong. That is why it is so surprising that we spend an inordinate amount of time separating one from another, judging people, blaming people, and casting people out of our 'in group' because they do not fit, for whatever reason.

I love Luke's Gospel because is an invitation to meet Jesus and Luke's Jesus is a man worth meeting as he mixes with the dregs of Jewish society, at least in the eyes of the Religious people. Luke always has Jesus situated with those who are on the edges and he challenges us to let go of all our attempts to be good religious people and invites us to open our hearts to the poor and the broken. He invites us to be real. It is the most scandalising piece of writing because it says that in God's eyes, all are of value and all are welcome. By God's very nature, God is inclusive and not exclusive. Even our trinitarian theology says as much. We worship one God in three persons. Our theology of creation reminds us of that truth as the blueprint of the universe invites us to recognise that everything is pointing us towards unity and inclusivity. That means, of course, in our eyes, every person has to be of value and welcome. That challenges us to become people who are inclusive rather than exclusive.

When I was a university chaplain many years ago, I used to take groups of students to visit the Poor Clares when they were in Liverpool. There is a little bit of mystique surrounding enclosed orders and the students were always fascinated by the sisters' lifestyle. It seemed to many of them a real waste of time to shut yourself off from the world and pray for the world.

I always found it interesting how the buzz of chatter on the minibus would grind to a halt when we went through the gates to the monastery which would shut behind us. We were then taken to the parlour by a silent extern sister. Here we waited for the other sisters to arrive. I think the students wondered if we would ever get out.

On one visit the sisters came into the parlour and began to introduce themselves. There was one ancient looking lady who beamed around at us all and introduced herself as Sister Mary Francis. Almost as one, the other sisters turned around to her and said, 'No you are not'. It was very funny at the time and obviously the sister in question had some problems, but it has made me think how so few of us really know who we are. Very few of us know the truth that we are beloved children of God and therefore it is safe to face ourselves and allow change and transformation to happen. You know God's love for us is everlasting. The Scriptures say it over and over. God's love for us existed before we were born and will exist after we have died. There has never been a time when you have not been loved. It matters not what you have done or not done. You will always be loved perfectly. It is an eternal love in which we are embraced. It is the heart of God, the action of God the reality of God. Nothing to do with deserving or not deserving. Spirituality is, in part, about claiming that eternal love for ourselves so that we can live our lives in love for God and for each other.

As I have written before, the temple of Jesus day played a huge role in the life of the God-fearing Jew. It was the centre of the economic system, the political system the social system and of course the Religious system. Those who were allowed to worship held the power in all those areas. According to the law, and particularly in the book of Leviticus, there were huge numbers of people excluded from temple worship who were therefore outside the systems that made Jewish society work.

The profoundly radical nature of Luke's Gospel is that Luke's Jesus will sit down and share food with the outsider. He becomes an icon of the inclusive nature of God. Whoever lives on the edges of the systems that made Jewish society work - lepers, prostitutes, gentiles, even public sinners - are Jesus' friends. By mixing with them, Jesus makes himself, in the eyes of the Jewish authorities, unclean and outside the system. It is clear that Luke's Jesus is saying to anyone who is willing to listen, that no one is unacceptable, that no-one is irredeemable, that no one is excluded.

He must have been the most frustrating of men because he never did what was expected. He was hardly ever seen with the respectable people. In a Church that seems to be a community for those who are acceptable and who live in a seemingly acceptable way, maybe we have some lessons to learn from Luke's Jesus about inclusion.

I was reading recently something that Ronald Rolheiser the Canadian Oblate priest wrote. It made a lot of sense to me. He wrote that our arrival in this world is categorised by loneliness, separation and a sense of being cut off from that which gives us life, namely our mothers. The absolute shock of birth means that every part of us aches, consciously and unconsciously, sensing that we are incomplete, lonely, and cut off. Deep in our psyche we know that we are a little piece of matter that was once part of something bigger than we are. Those feelings mean that in a sense we are all on the edges and desperately seeking to belong to something bigger than ourselves. I guess, the truth is that we are all damaged and broken as we try to make sense of the trauma of separation. The salvation of God can only really be understood when we are in touch with that ultimate poverty and are aware that only the Gospel can fulfil our need.

Sadly, most of us try to cover up our innate brokenness. We put in place systems of our own making to appear to be in control and to have it altogether. We refuse to recognise brokenness and vulnerability in our own lives so how can we recognise it in the lives of others? Luke's Jesus will challenge us to open our hearts and minds to our own need and to those who do not fit the norm.

As I have said, I was a university chaplain many years ago. I was invited to dinner with a couple of students who were very involved in the chaplaincy. I have to say, I was not looking forward to it. Student houses are often not the cleanest of places and food is necessarily of the cheapest variety and not always plentiful. When I arrived, I met Tony and Anna who had been invited along too. Anna was studying to be a doctor and professed no faith in God at all. Tony was a law student who said that, at best, he was agnostic. They were lovely young people, but it was only when the conversation developed that I realised just how lovely they were. The surroundings and the food faded into insignificance as I listened to these two, with a bit of prompting, talk about their lives. It seemed, they spent most of their spare time working around Liverpool, trying to make a difference to the poor and needy. Anna spent a lot of time putting her medical training to good use. She went around night shelters and bandaged wounds and gave advice on health matters. She even badgered newly qualified doctors to help those that she was unable to care for. Tony volunteered in soup kitchens and also went out at night on soup runs trying to help those who were desperately hungry and for whatever reason lived on the streets.

They were an extraordinary pair and I felt very humbled by all they did. I knew that in them I was meeting the risen Christ. Whether they saw it or not, for me, they were the risen Jesus as they reached out to those in need. Yet again it seemed to me that they were Christ for those that they worked with, and made a difference to.

There was a process that the Gospels went through to be put together in the form we have them. As I have said before they are not biographies of Jesus, meant to give an historical basis for belief. They are faith stories meant to invite us to relationship with him, so that we might believe. The word Synoptic means to see with the same eyes. Luke uses a lot of the same material as Mark and Matthew, but he gives it a different emphasis changing words here and there to make his own points. It is those changes and the extra material that we find which enable us to see what Luke's biases were and to identify the concerns that his Community had.

What do we know about Luke? He is a gentile or a non-Jew. Scholars tell us that he was possibly a Syrian or a Roman and was almost certainly a convert to Christianity. He is also very well educated. His text is well written and influenced strongly by contemporary culture. It is obvious from his text that Luke has read Mark's Gospel which was probably written between 55 and 65AD. Almost one third of his text comes from Mark. The rest of it is from a document that the Scholars think must have existed which we call Q.

Luke has several main themes running through his Gospel. It is these themes that help us understand Luke's Jesus. His Gospel is a missionary document. Luke's community is obviously concerned to spread the Good News. People are always being sent out. That's a call which is still necessary today and to which people are still responding. It is obvious that new ways of proclaiming the Gospel have to be found because the old ways are finished and done. Pope Francis has written 'I dream of a 'missionary option', that is, a missionary impulse capable of transforming everything, so that the church's customs, ways of doing things, times and schedules, language and structures can be suitably channelled for the evangelisation of today's world rather than for her self-preservation.' Luke's understanding is that it has to be the Gospel of inclusion and forgiveness and mercy and compassion that is spread. It seems so sad that we as Church often miss opportunities to be inclusive and merciful.

Luke's perspective is much wider than either Matthew or Mark. By his time Christians have made the break with Judaism and have begun to see themselves as something different. Luke is not afraid of offending the Jewish Christians. He is a little like a convert to Catholicism, who does not have the same hang ups that the rest of us have. Luke's Jesus does not shy away from the difficult places and the difficult conversation. He simply sees the need to proclaim the all-inclusive goodness of God.

Luke is the most broad-minded and the most forgiving of the evangelists and so the Jesus he presents is broadminded and forgiving. Every chance he gets, Luke has Jesus forgiving people, right up to the good thief on the cross. It pervades almost every story he tells. There seems to be no limit to God's mercy; all are called to salvation - the poor, social outcasts, the gentiles. It is inclusivity again!

Women in the Palestine of Jesus day were treated as the property of men and had no rights whatsoever, but we find Luke bringing women into Jesus' life. More than that he shows Jesus' unique way of relating to women who are always portrayed in a good light. Luke presents them as competent, sensible and valuable. They are shown as faithful disciples who remain with Jesus right up to Calvary. It was to the women that the message of the resurrection was given. This was so shocking to the Jews of Jesus' day.

He balances any story or parable that has a man at its centre with one dealing with a woman. The man with the hundred sheep in chapter 15 is followed by the woman with ten drachmas. Jesus raises the widow's son at Nain and later he goes on to raise the daughter of Jairus. It is that beautiful comprehensive under-standing of the nature of God.

Throughout the gospel we become aware that Luke knows that Jesus is not going to return in glory in the next few years and so the theology he develops takes that into account. He is beginning to tease out what that might mean. Luke frequently mentions the Spirit and his thrust is that we are living in the age of the Spirit. His emphasis is not on the return of Jesus but on the outpouring of the Spirit. He wants us to know that those who call on the Spirit and rely upon the Spirit will live in the new age. Luke is preoccupied and filled with a sense of the Spirit. For Luke the Spirit is behind everything. That means Luke's Jesus is a man prompted and led by the Spirit of God as he reveals the truth of love in the heart of God for all people.

Luke also wants us to know that the Kingdom is here, now, and his cry is, we must rejoice in it and live in it. Try not to worry about the final days. It is an academic question to worry about when the historical Jesus will return. His risen presence is with us now. The text is filled with a sense of God's imminence and with the necessity to see and be aware. Today is the day of salvation, so today is the moment of grace. Jesus lives very much in the present in this Gospel and discovers the presence of God in good and bad alike. I guess most of us could do with learning that lesson.

Another major theme we will find is the call we are given to renounce everything. To be a disciple means we have to renounce everything not just money or external possessions but inner idols and the concerns of the ego. In order to be like the Jesus that Luke presents to us we have to be willing to let go. Most of us hold on to much that we do not need. In order to live as Luke's Jesus lives, we have to be able to embrace all people regardless of the categories we put on them.

Luke uses every story he can to show that what impresses God does not necessarily impress people. He reminds us that people who think they are on the top are often on the bottom and those who think they are on the bottom are on the top in God's eyes. There is no place for power or domination, which the world thinks brings success. Luke sees the Christian community as a co-operative system of service, sharing, caring for the poor, giving away of surplus possessions. It is a real upside-down theology and it is why Luke's writing is often called the Gospel of the poor. As part of this bias towards the bottom strata of society, Luke presents Jesus advocating a new social pattern. This is a much more horizontal pattern than the hierarchy of exploitation and domination of his day which is not that different from our own. In Jesus' eyes, all people are equal, and he treats them as such. I think it is fair to say that Jesus became a threat to the political system of his day simply because he helped people see themselves differently.

Throughout Luke's Gospel we find many passages which deal with non-violence. Jesus' death is itself a teaching on how to absorb the pain of violence by taking it into himself and triumphing over it by love. To admit it, would mean that we have to be non-violent too. Luke's Jesus invites us to look at the violence in our own lives. We can be extraordinarily violent in the language we use and the patterns of thought that we have about various groups of people. We need to reflect on Jesus teaching of non-violence.

Luke is also convinced of the absoluteness of God's reign. Whenever he faces authority in his exchanges with Pilate or Herod, he tells them the truth about who reigns, who is the absolute power. You can begin to see why it is such a radical powerful document. It is on the side of the oppressed and it challenges much of the world's view on life.

I would like to spend the rest of this chapter reflecting on the infancy narratives, the stories that surround the birth of Jesus. What happens? Joseph and Mary go to Bethlehem. The trip might well be a Lucan creation. So, it is important to ask ourselves what he is trying to tell us theologically. The prophet Micah seems to say that the messiah will be born in Bethlehem and so Luke has to make that happen. The word Bethlehem means 'house of bread' and Luke shows us that Jesus will become the bread of life for us. He will be our nourishing food. When the child was born Mary swaddles her son. The swaddling clothes were baby wraps. She then puts him in a manger again symbolic because a manger was the animal's food box.

Nick Page, who is one of the most interesting of Christian authors around at the moment, would challenge us to move from our traditional understanding of the birth of Jesus. We presume that

Mary was sent away from every dwelling in Bethlehem when looking for a place to give birth. He says that, culturally, Joseph's family home would have been the first place for Mary to give birth. It would have been a crowded household with little space in the 'Kataluma', which means inn or guest room. They laid the baby elsewhere in the house, probably the only place where there was space, the animals' lodgings.

What Nick Page seems to be saying is that Jesus from the very moment of his birth was made welcome, that Mary was not shunned even though there would have been whispering about her and the baby. This inclusivity which is at the core of the Torah, or Jewish law, was right there at the beginning of Jesus life. Is it any wonder then that it is at the core of his ministry?

Then the angel of the Lord looks for the shepherds in the fields. They were social and religious outcasts. If Luke were writing today, the good news would have been announced to a group of winos or drug addicts. These people were not romantic figures they were dirty, unsociable, smelly and spent more time communicating with sheep than anything else.

The angel of the Lord says to the shepherds, 'To you is born a saviour' indicating that Jesus is God's gift to those who are of no worth in society. Here we have Gospel inclusivity yet again. The shepherds then tell everyone about what has happened. They are a reminder to us that it is through the likes of them that the message will be proclaimed. It reminds us too that it is the message that is important, not the messenger. How often do we look at the messenger rather than the message?

Mary ponders all that happens. It is a reminder to us of the importance of reflection in life if we are to understand the presence of God in our midst. Mary has to work at understanding who her son is and holds it all until it makes sense.

The presentation of Jesus in the Temple closes the infancy narratives. It reminds us of the scene in the first book of Samuel. Yet another parallel. Mary makes the offering of the poor two turtledoves for her purification. Simeon the prophet rejoices in the birth of the Messiah but reminds Mary that her heart will be pierced by a sword which in Jewish imagery is that which divides and separates. That is what will happen in the life of this child. He will divide and separate by what he says and what he does as he reaches out to those who are broken and in need.

We also have the appearance of Anna who symbolises the faithful ones waiting for the coming of the Messiah. The infancy narratives end with an emphasis on Jesus growing up physically and in an understanding of who he is. It is true therefore that if he grew in understanding of himself, he grew in understanding of God and of his call to the world. Luke adds one more scene where Jesus himself declares who he is and why he came. Luke is the only one who gives us a scene from the hidden life of Jesus. The story has Jesus supposedly lost in the Temple. After Mary finds him, she tells him off, but Jesus reminds her and Joseph of his true origins and his true Father. It is again a created story to remind us that Jesus has a mission to undergo. This all too human Jesus has a divine nature and lest we forget, Luke wants to remind us.

The last scene of the infancy narrative links with the final scene of the gospel as a whole. Luke places a strong emphasis on journeys throughout his gospel. This journey has similarities with the final journey to Jerusalem in which Jesus travels up for the Passover with his disciples, his new family. In both accounts, the time of 'three days' is significant. On both occasions Jesus is 'lost' for three days and both times he is about his Father's business. This is business that creates a new world order as Jesus inspires us to reach out to the broken, the lost, the insignificant, and the forgotten. In doing that he reveals the heart of God to the world. When we become like Jesus, we too reveal the heart of God to the world, a heart of all-embracing love.

EIGHT

MORE THAN WE DESERVE

My mum died of cancer 26 years ago. I will never forget the day that the specialists told me what was wrong with her. I then had to go and tell mum that she was dying. I sat at her bedside in the hospital and she asked me what the specialist had said. I told her that she had cancer and she looked at me and said, 'I am not going to get better am I?' My only response, as the tears began to fall, was to stammer out the word 'No'. She then asked a typical question, 'How long have I got?' and I was unable to answer her. We sat and cried for a bit and then she asked me to leave her.

I came back later that day and mum was sitting up in bed with her make up on and a fresh nightdress. I looked at her and smiled and I realised in looking at her that was a real choice for life. She then told me that she was going to live the time that she had left. Her way of living was to come out of hospital and give away all the material things in her life that she had built up over 68 years so that she was then free to concentrate on the real things of life.

Over the next weeks, she reflected on compassion, forgiveness, relationship and love. She told the people who mattered to her that she loved them. She did this, not just in words, but in a whole number of ways, even in the giving of her ornaments and pictures. I will never forget watching her sitting with her friend of over 40 years and saying to me, 'This is life.'

I believe she spoke truth in those words. All we really have, when the chips are down, is love, and the compassion, forgiveness, brokenness, and vulnerability that go with it. All we have is our relationship with God, with ourselves and with one another and they are all inter-twined. Discover God and you will find the reality of yourself. Discover yourself and you will find God who lives in you. Discover another person and you will find God and yourself. What did my mum do to deserve such wisdom? Nothing. Why was she able to see so clearly? I suppose, it was because of a life-time of faith. Why was she filled with such peace and understood that God was by her side? I do not know, other than to believe that is all gift and it is all so much more than we deserve.

As I said in the last chapter, Luke's Gospel is often called the upside-down Gospel because it constantly turns the world's values on their head. I guess in many senses the whole of the Scriptures do that, but Luke does it supremely well as he has Jesus reveal the face of God to us.

One of the central truths that the Bible turns upside down is the justice of God. In the Scriptures, justice is God being true to Godself. God's justice is unconditional love because for God to be true to God's self is to be faithful to unconditional love. And so Luke's Gospel is filled with images of God's justice in the Scriptural sense. We find Jesus eating with tax collectors and sinners. He heals the woman with the haemorrhage. He encounters Zaccheus, the hated tax collector, and transforms his life. He is invited to parties and banquets that are for everyone who listens to the good news of God's justice. All of these people had to be in Luke's Gospel because of the unconditional nature of God's love that Luke wants to reveal to us. He tells stories to illustrate the truth of that unconditional love, the Prodigal son or the forgiving Father, the woman with her lost coin, shepherds looking for sheep.

God's justice always gives us more than we deserve. You see, what the Scriptures are telling us is that life is not about being worthy and clean and righteous. We are never any of those things and we never will be. It is about being open to God's unconditional love; and so all through Luke's Gospel people are given more than they deserve. It is a revolution in understanding the nature of God. It turns every system we operate by upside down.

I first met Aggie when she worked at the local Spar shop. Whenever I went in to the shop I would be greeted with the customary, 'Hello love'. I saw her at events with the 'Hasbeens', a local music group, and at various occasions around the town of Southport. When I became parish priest in the town, some years later, I heard that Aggie was looking for a job and she came, and she stayed. I could write about the laughter she brought. Wherever Aggie went there was so much laughter but actually what Aggie taught me was so much deeper. She taught me about unconditional love and amazing generosity. She went far above and beyond her job, as a housekeeper, in working with the poor. She fed hundreds at the door and found clothes and furniture for them. She was a Eucharistic minister reaching out to the sick and the lonely. There is one story, however, which spoke volumes to me about Aggie, her love of God and her trust in God. Aggie was always larger than life and as blunt as they make them. Many people experienced a listening ear and a good dollop of common sense delivered 'Aggie style' when they came to our door.

It was the end of a long hard day and we had a crowd of people needing food. There was nothing left, and Aggie stood in the middle of the room and in a loud voice said 'Lord these are your people and they are hungry. What are you going to do about it?' Virtually as she finished the prayer the door-bell went and one of the local bakers stood there with a tray full of bread and pies freshly made. He had heard about what we were doing and thought he might be able to help. Aggie was not a bit surprised. I was, but she trusted that God would do what God would do, a woman of faith who never doubted her God even if at times she did not understand what God was doing. A woman who, by the life she lived, had become God's unconditional love because she knew God's unconditional love.

So, what do I mean by justice? God's justice is not about retaliation or punishment; it is about facing reality and doing whatever we can to change that reality for the good. This is the kind of restorative justice we are promised to receive from God. Whatever has happened in our lives, ultimately God will restore us and make us whole. So Christian justice is about restoration. It is about making whole. The justice we desire is that which heals and restores humanity. It is the justice that comes from a loving heart and which transforms the world we live in.

Every human being is inherently and equally good. Remember that wonderful phrase that the author of the book of Genesis uses, 'God saw that it was good.' We have dignity. We are worthy of respect. Having said that, we seem unable to ignore our very real differences and our egotistical nature makes value judgements based on those differences. Richard Rohr says, 'Arbitrary, artificial hierarchies and discrimination are based on a variety of differences: for example, gender, sexuality, class, skin colour, education, physical or mental ability, attractiveness, accent, language, religion, and so on.' Sadly, some people are seen as good, and others as less good. God's justice demands that all people everywhere are treated with dignity and respect despite their differences because that is the justice of God. Remember the story that Luke's Jesus tells of the labourers in the vineyard. Each one is paid the same regardless of how long they have spent working. To bring God's justice to bear on the world we have, always and everywhere, to call attention to imbalances of privilege and power. That is the abundance of God's life being poured out onto the world. That is God's justice coming to bear on the world.

Sadly, what we have had for most of history, is largely 'retributive justice'. We seem to want to punish people for what they do wrong. We want to make them pay. Ronald Rolheiser once wrote, 'I do not deny the existence of hell, nor of the importance of

God's judgment, but the itch to see other people suffer retribution reveals things about ourselves that we might not want to admit.' I think it is true that we often make God in our image and likeness in order to justify our own need for revenge and retribution. We sometimes use the death of Jesus to justify our need for punishment of those who do wrong. Jesus died on the cross, we say, and took our punishment. It is Richard Rohr who says, 'It is time for Christianity to rediscover the real biblical theme of restorative justice, which focuses on rehabilitation, healing, and reconciliation, not punishment. We should call Jesus' story the 'myth of redemptive suffering' - not as in 'paying a price' but as in offering the self for the other. 'At-one-ment' instead of atonement!'

In Isaiah 58:1-9, Isaiah explores what justice may be when he says that God prefers a kind of fasting which changes our actual lifestyle and not just punishes our body. Isaiah makes a very upfront demand for social justice, non-aggression, taking our feet off the necks of the oppressed, sharing our bread with the hungry, clothing the naked, sheltering the homeless, letting go of our sense of entitlement, and not speaking maliciously. He says very clearly this is the real fast God wants.

Justice is to be at the core of our understanding of mercy and our desire to let God's abundant life flow into the world. Luke's Jesus reveals the justice of God because he is true to himself and therefore can only be the love that he has experienced in the heart of God. Luke's Jesus is constantly merciful because it is God being true to Godself. No wonder his encounters and the stories that he tells invite a radical, revolutionary change of heart and mind. I think the truth is that many of us find the Jesus that Luke reveals very difficult to handle. All our worldly systems, despite what we say of them, are based on retributive justice and that is all most of us want. We want God to be like us and indulge us in our petty need for revenge and God is other, always giving more than we deserve.

Many years ago, when I was studying to be a priest, I opted to do some prison work as a pastoral placement. I have no idea what made me do it and other students thought it was madness. When I walk into prisons these days, I know that God was preparing my heart and my mind all those years ago. We all had to go through an induction process. As we walked onto one of the wings, the experienced officer we had with us advised us always to walk to one or other side of the corridor. He said you could never be sure what prisoners would throw from other landings. He walked on with us following. Then he stopped, and he said to us with a real sense of anger both in his voice and on his face that the vast majority of prisoners should not be held captive because they had mental health issues. He said that most of them should be receiving psychiatric care. He had a wry smile on his face when he said something like, 'But society demands its pound of flesh.' What a sad indictment on humanity and on our society, that we would choose to punish rather than heal those who hurt us.

Ronald Rolheiser recently wrote in his one of his weekly meditations that, 'God is not a God of punishment, but a God of forgiveness'. Right at the heart of Luke's Gospel is the power of forgiveness. He went on to say, 'God is not a God who records our sins, but a God who washes them away.' I love Luke's account of the paralytic, lowered through the roof by his friends. What does Jesus say to him? 'Your sins are forgiven'. Rolheiser then wrote, 'God is not a God who demands perfection from us, but a God who asks for a contrite heart when we cannot measure up'. Read Luke's story about the tax collector and the Pharisee. Then Rolheiser said something extraordinary, 'God is not a God who gives us only one chance, but a God who gives us infinite chances.' There it is, the heart of the revelation of God that Luke's Jesus gives us, unconditional love, infinite chances. He then reminds us that God is a God who comes searching for us, full of understanding and care. Remember the crazy shepherd who goes looking for the one sheep that is lost. The next phrase Rolheiser uses is beautiful: 'God is not a God who is calculating and parsimonious in his gifts, but a prodigal God who sows seeds everywhere without regard for waste or worthiness.' God's love is abundant and lavish as God desires our restoration and renewal. Rolheiser then said that, 'God not a God who is powerless before evil and death, but a God who can raise dead bodies to life and redeem what is evil and hopeless.' Luke's Jesus dies on the cross trusting and believing in the goodness of God who will turn all things to good. God always pours out on us far more than we ever deserve.

The presumption in Luke's Gospel is that what we have received we will share. Luke wants to show us that it is possible to be truly human and truly just if we live in the power of the Spirit and so the Spirit is central in the Gospel. It is the Spirit that gives us the power to love unconditionally. Unconditional love is a good test of how full of the Spirit we are. It is the Spirit that gives us the power to be compassionate and caring and forgiving. It is the Spirit that gives us the power to trust. That is why Luke will tell us to ask for the Spirit if we want to be like Jesus.

At Irenaeus, the project I work for, we are engaged in helping to train Eucharistic Ministers for the Archdiocese of Liverpool. For those who are not of the Catholic tradition, these are people who are trained to give out Holy Communion at Mass. Some time back, I was helping at just such a day of training. During one of the sessions, the woman I was working with began to tell a story about the death of her best friend's mother. It was Holy Week and, on the Thursday morning, Maureen received a phone call asking her to drop everything and go to her friend's mum's house.

When she got to the house, everyone was distraught. The woman had died, suddenly, after having a massive haemorrhage. Her body was in such a terrible state the ambulance men had removed it immediately. Maureen went up to the bedroom and saw the state of the bed and the room and knew that she could not leave it like that. So, she began to scrub the walls and the carpet in the midst of her own tears and pain at the death of someone she had loved very much. She said it was while she was doing that, for the first time in her life she understood the presence of the Spirit in our lives. There was no way that she could do such a loving thing without the energy of God that inspired her and motivated her. When she had finished, she went downstairs and cooked a meal for those who were there and left it for them. Sometimes the unconditional love of God can be seen in the extraordinary things we do, that we consider to be nothing exceptional.

In the last half of chapter 6, we find Luke's beatitudes. I want to spend some time, in this chapter, reflecting on them because they reveal something to us of Luke's Jesus. They are an attempt to describe what it is like to live the happy life, the freed life, the life that is in touch. Unlike Matthew's Gospel, Luke's beatitudes are addressed to disciples. Remember Matthew has Jesus, like the new Moses, going up the mountain and once his disciples have sat down with him, he addresses the crowd. Luke has Jesus come down the mountain and, fixing his eyes on his disciples, begins to speak. He is describing to disciples what it means to be a Disciple and so his beatitudes are much more direct and even confrontational than Matthew's eight beatitudes. It reminds us that Luke's Jesus is never afraid to put himself in the firing line and invites controversy and misunderstanding.

Luke's beatitudes are addressed to those who are already committed to Jesus' way and they give instances of what happens when the Kingdom of God comes upon the world. Luke's beatitudes speak of what happens when people get involved in God's way of doing things but there is a promise that God can handle the mess and ultimately transform it so that we are blessed in the midst of it all.

If we are the disciples of Jesus, then we will know the truth that we are blessed when we are facing the poverty of rejection and frustration. We will know that we are blessed when we hunger for what is right and true. We will experience blessing when we weep for those who are broken and in pain. We are blessed when we know that, without God, we cannot live fully human lives.

Many years ago, I met a woman who has since become a life-long friend. Her early life was quite difficult. She never knew her father although she had met him on occasion. When her mother married, her stepfather did not want Louise hanging around and so she was packed off to live with her aunt and uncle and then her grandparents. When she was twelve, she went back to her mum and stepfather and I guess because she had been shunted around an awful lot was very difficult to handle. At such a young age she got into drugs and alcohol abuse. She was eventually sent to boarding school and was just as much trouble there.

When she was 15 and on the verge of being expelled, she found herself in the head teacher's office. For the first time in her life he asked her a question that no one else had ever asked. He wanted to know what was wrong. Louise said that it was like a dam bursting as all her pain, her rejection, her insecurity and her fear came flooding out. The head teacher, who was a man of faith, prayed with her and as she cried away some of her pain, she recognised within herself a new peace. She says now that she knew for the first time that Jesus was real. That led her into a deep appreciation of her humanity and the gift of life.

That encounter with the head teacher transformed her but brought her into more conflict than she had ever experienced before. Her very rich family disinherited her as she began to take the Gospel more and more seriously. They could not cope with the person who went to Church most days and whose compassion and humanity caused her to work with the homeless. They were unable able to handle her political involvement which was quite radical and focused always on the needs of others. They could not cope with the person who no longer judged and criticised others, nor with the person who began to live simply and for whom prayer was important. More than anything, they found it very difficult to deal with someone who by her own lifestyle questioned theirs. Louise had discovered what it meant to be human and alive in the way that Luke's Jesus helps us to see what it means. Is that an easy road to travel? Absolutely not but it the most fulfilling way to live our lives.

It is interesting that Luke only has four beatitudes and couples them with four statements about the state of the world. Alas for you who are rich now. Alas for you who have your fill now. Alas for you who laugh now. Alas for you when people speak well of you. It is as though he is saying to the Disciples, do not lose yourself in things that are passing away things that do not last. The question Luke wants us to ask ourselves when faced with this is, What is God all about? What lasts in life? What is real?

At the end of the Beatitudes is possibly the most challenging request. 'Love your enemies, do good to those who hate you, bless those who curse you, pray for those who treat you badly' This is absurd teaching. It is an impossible request and unless you have really responded to eternal life, you will not see its value. I love the words of St Thomas More when he faced the judges who condemned him. He said: 'I verily trust and shall therefore right heartily pray that though your Lordships have now here on earth been judges to my condemnation, we may hereafter in heaven merrily all meet together to our everlasting salvation.'

That sort of attitude is not achievable by ourselves, but only in the power of God can we find the strength to be all that Disciples are called to be. That is why all the time Luke will reflect on the Spirit and invite us to be filled with the power of the Spirit to overflowing so that we can love. Luke's Jesus is never afraid of the hard word or the challenging reality of love because he lives it within himself.

A few years ago, a Vicar in South London hit the headlines for attempting to make his service more relevant for the young people in his area by using Rap Music and contemporary dancing and lighting. There was uproar amongst some of his parishioners who seemed to think that what he was doing was an outrage and talked of the sanctity of ancient hymns and even more ancient language.

I remember reading an article in the Tablet from a right wing politician in South America who criticised the Church for being involved in the struggle of the poor, and basically said the Church should be concerned with singing hymns and saying prayers but not be involved in the day to day living of people.

The sort of attitudes exhibited by both the parishioners in South London and the right wing politician seem to me to be in direct

conflict with the way in which Luke's Jesus lived. He used
contemporary issues to get his point across. He was involved with
the real issues that people struggled with. He fed the poor. He
raised the dead. He mixed with the outcasts. He forgave those
who needed it. He stood against the systems and power structures
of his day that would ensnare people. His kingdom was not *of*
this world, but it was *for* this world and for eternity, a kingdom
of justice and truth and love and forgiveness. To live in that
kingdom is more than we deserve and yet we live in that
kingdom, if we choose to, because of the benevolence of God

NINE
CALLED TO SERVE

Railway stations are strange places particularly on a cold, grey, dank morning with the sort of drizzle falling that soaks everyone alike. Full of cold grey people going about their business interacting with no one, they are magnets for the lost and the lonely, the stranger and the strange who fade into the grey nothingness without explanation.

Station waiting rooms are just the same. Anonymous people hiding behind newspapers say little to one another for fear it might break the monotony. Here too are the stranger and the strange, the lost and the lonely, huddled into their corners wishing their lives away. It was here that the drama was played out. They came in, the little woman and her charge. Nothing extraordinary, wet from the rain, the wheelchair leaving huge puddles as it squeaked across the dirty linoleum, the little woman panting from the exertion of pushing. She found a seat and sat with the chair facing her.

Into the drab colourless waiting room came life as the little woman and her charge laughed and touched one another with the sort of wordless communication that only comes between those who share their lives with one another. The woman brought out a towel and gently and lovingly, dried the girl in the chair. She brought out food, fed her and gave her a drink which slaked her thirst. She held her hands and smiled and laughed and the girl responded crowing with delight as she looked into the eyes of the little woman who loved her. Time stood still as in her actions we saw what was important in life and what was important brought meaning into what was often a meaningless place.

It was time to go then, not for me but for them. They squeaked back across the floor and out into the cold and it seemed as though the light had gone out, and yet there was a light within me because I knew that I had seen something extraordinary. They never came again, the little woman and the girl, although I looked for them. The following Sunday in my local Church I celebrated the Eucharist and knew that what I was doing ritually I had done in a railway waiting room with two people who had given their lives to each other and brought life to others because of it. It is strange what you can see in a railway station if you open your eyes and look.

I think that is a wonderful story of love and service. I was reflecting recently on the sacrament of baptism and was reading a book about baptism being the ritual setting apart for service. I have written about this before, but I think it is true to say that most of us look at life with a dualistic mind. We divide and separate rather than see the whole. That is why so many of us blame, judge and scapegoat others, because we see them through a dualistic mindset. The Jesus, Luke presents to us, never did that, which is why he could share food with those called sinners and those called Pharisees, seemingly opposite ends of the pole. He simply looked for goodness and did not categorise people by what they did or did not do.

I think because of our dualistic mindset, every aspect of our thinking and feeling is affected, even our spiritual lives. Some things become holy and other things are not holy because they are not graced with the presence of God. Church becomes the holy place which necessarily means that other places are not holy. Some people become holy. So, priests, deacons, monks, nuns, leaders and those who practice religion piously are holy. That again means there are others who are not holy. We set apart altars, certain dishes and clothing and they become holy and are treated with great respect when nothing else is. The word consecration, that is sometimes used in religious circles can mean to set apart for service rather than to separate for some specifically religious purpose.

One of my favourite characters in the first, or old, testament is Moses. He was consecrated or set apart for service. I love the imagery in his story, the burning bush, the plagues, walls of water to the right and the left, the chariots of Pharaoh; but ultimately, I love the triumph of good over evil. When God called Moses to leave his lovely, quiet life as a shepherd and go to Pharaoh and ask him to set his people, the Israelites, free, Moses struggles with the command. He does not want to do what he is called to do. He tries to get God to send his brother, Aaron. If you read the story it is a wonderful illustration of how we, human beings, pass the buck. Moses tells God that Aaron was able to speak clearly without a stammer. He had good leadership qualities. He would be much, much better at doing the job. However, Aaron had not seen the suffering of God's people in the way that Moses had. More than that even, he had not felt the suffering of God's people in the way that Moses had, and because of that it had to be Moses. Moses cannot walk away because he has seen, and felt, what the people of Israel have gone through and so he is the one set apart, the one who is not free to walk away. The circumstances of his life and the need of his people have set him apart. It is a call that is mirrored through the ancient stories we read in the Bible. Jeremiah is called and he does not want to go but he has to because he has been given the word that will set his people free. Jonah, another reluctant prophet, does not want to go and do what he has to do, but go he must and so he finally preaches to the Ninevites. Isaiah protests his unworthiness; David is too young. The list goes on of people who are consecrated, set apart not to be seen as holy, in our often narrow understanding, but to serve God's people.

Ronald Rolheiser shares that our basic understanding of church has at its heart this concept of being set apart. The word Ecclesia comes from two Greek words: 'Ek Kaleo'. 'Ek' means, 'out of'; and 'Kaleo' means, 'to be called'. So, to be a member of the Church is to be 'called out of'. You might wonder what is it that we are called out of or away from? It is whatever we would be doing if we were not part of the church. It is to be called out of whatever might have formed our lives had we not been baptised and called to discipleship. Baptism and church membership set us apart for service in much the same way as Moses, Jeremiah, Jonah, Mary, Joseph, indeed Jesus himself were set apart and called to live a life of service. Ronald Rolheiser says, 'The needs and wounds of our world are constantly asking us to suspend our radical freedom, to set aside our own agendas, in order to serve.' Like

Moses and the others, we cannot walk away. Luke's Jesus challenges us to serve, not to relegate our Baptism to some sort of cultic reality but to know it sets us apart to view the world holistically and to find a way of serving the pain and brokenness of God's people.

Through our Baptism we are all called to serve so I would like to spend some time in this chapter reflecting on our Baptism. Desmond Tutu, the South African Archbishop has often said that he has only one message. The message is simple and repeated over and over again. He says this message is the heart of the Gospel and here it is, in his own words, 'God loves you'. He goes on to say, 'I tell them that, because the entire culture tells them they are unlovable, and I have to give them the message of who they really are, children of God, loved by him.'

Jesus' baptism tells us very clearly who he is in the sight of God, when he hears the words, 'This is my son, the beloved'. He discovered that he was loved by God in a deeply intimate way. Our baptism is meant to do the same. It reminds us and the world that we are beloved children of God. It is almost a public declaration of that truth. We have been invested with the most incredible dignity as God's children. It is a reminder too, of course, that we should be defined by God and not by others. Sadly, this is not always the case. This wonderful reality, can all too easily be forgotten in the culture we live in. We are bombarded with pressures and advertisements that tell us we should change our image, change our job, earn more money. We are under pressure to be better sexually or physically or both. If much of the advertising in the modern world is to be believed, we are called to be beautiful and to feel good about ourselves. We are nothing if we are merely ourselves. We must be other, and more than that. Our baptism tells us clearly that this is nonsense because God has loved us and created us as we are, and we are wonderful human beings.

If our baptism defines us as being in relationship to God because we are named as children of that God, it also defines our relationship with one another. In the words of the Sister Sledge song, 'We are family'. We pray 'Our Father' not 'my father'. We belong together as children of God. In my Catholic tradition, whenever we enter the Church, we are encouraged to sign ourselves with water to remind us of our Baptism. It is a reminder that we belong to God, not just privately, but publicly, openly. It makes a statement that we are God's beloved son, God's beloved daughter and therefore that we belong to one another.

When Jesus heard those extraordinary words, 'You are my beloved', he knew that he was called to be the friend of the outcast, the sinner, the broken, and the confused. That meant that he had to become one of the great hordes in Jewish society who were at times unacceptable for temple worship and therefore outside the system. God's people needed to be set free. Jesus was called to let humanity know that God delights is us, not because we are good, bad or indifferent but because we are God's delight. It is all God's initiative.

We are called to share in that ministry, to walk with those who live on the edges, and who at times are seen as unacceptable and tell them that God delights in them. Richard Rohr invites us to reflect on who we are called to when he says, 'The poor, prisoners, immigrants, homeless, addicts, and those who are marginalised or hurting, often have a natural empathy and sympathy for one another. They know something together that the rest of us do not know. Baptism is supposed to be an initiation into sympathy and solidarity with this 'body,' but I am afraid it seldom is.'

Luke's Jesus is not a comfortable man to get to know because he challenges us to be like him and to serve the children of God because God delights in them as much as in us. I know that it is very easy to simply talk about the poor and ignore the rest of humanity that we are also called to serve. Having said that, Pope Francis during his pontificate, apart from the scandals he has had to face, has majored on talking about our mandate to serve the poor. If you look back in our tradition all the prophets taught, using typically rabbinic language and imagery, that God is on the side of the poor and that we will be judged according to the way in which we treat the poor.

The phrase 'orphans, widows, and strangers' that we read so often in the Bible, is scriptural short-hand for those who, at any given time, are the three most vulnerable groups in society. The scriptures also make the point that not only is God on the side of the weakest and most vulnerable in society, but God is in the poor. How we treat the poor is how we treat God. When I think of that it sends shivers down my spine. Watching the news and reading the papers at the moment can make a very sombre pastime. Just look at the agony on the faces of those who are forced to flee their homes and countries under unjust persecution and the threat of death. They have no place to go and no country or community to receive them. It is a terrible situation but, more than that, when we look at them, we are looking at God, and the way we respond to them is the way we respond to God. It is really frightening! As followers of Christ, we cannot turn our backs on them or turn them away. They are our brothers and sisters and it is more important that we respond to their needs than it is to be in Church each Sunday. It is stark and unambiguous when Jesus, in Matthew 25, says, 'When I was hungry...' When we stand before God, at the end of our lives, I think the only question we will be asked is, 'Did you love?'

One of the most valuable times in my life was spent when, as a parish priest, the community I was part of opened our hearts and minds to those who found themselves excluded from respectable society. Every emotion and attitude within me was challenged as I tried to respond to their needs. I had to face my own self-righteousness and my pre-conceived ideas. I had to overcome my revulsion and my selfishness. There were often occasions when I would want to shout at people who were difficult and uncomfortable to be with. I had to get over what other people thought of me and the looks I got when sitting with the alcoholics and the street people. They taught me so much. At times it was frustrating and thankless and at other times glorious and rewarding.

I often think of the time I spent working with people who,

through no real fault of their own, had found themselves living on the streets or in very poor bed and breakfast accommodation. I remember Simon who stuttered his way through life, feeling as though he had no real place in society. I remember Vin who had polio when he was young and who was left in the hospital by his parents who never returned, and who carried a huge chip on his shoulder. Nothing was ever good enough for him, not even the food and care he was offered. There was Rob who lived in an old car with his girlfriend Jo, the two of them always out for the one trick that would change their fortunes.

Patrick was one of my favourites. He wore a huge sheriff's hat and badge and carried everything he owned in his pockets. He was usually drunk but always polite. Alcohol had played a part in his life from the time he was a baby when his father would put Guinness in his bottle to make him sleep. Then there was big Mo and her kind, generous, laughing, daughter Pam, who was eventually murdered because of her addiction. Mo never recovered and was found dead in a bed-sit some months after her daughter's murder. John battled with alcoholism for most of his adult life. When his mother died there was nothing to stop him drinking and so he lost his house and spent all his days in a drunken stupor.

Russell was a heroin addict with a sparkle in his eye and a smile always hovering around his mouth who always hoped there would be more. He preferred to be in prison because at least there was chance of getting off drugs. Katie, who had been a psychiatric nurse, was an alcoholic and a sometimes prostitute living under

Southport pier. She would often arrive at our door having been badly beaten by a customer or a pimp and yet she would find the strength to tend to the wounds and needs of others.

When we began the project not everyone greeted it with enthusiasm. 'Why should we bother?', 'They disturb us'. 'What if they beat someone up or rob them?' 'They are conning you' I heard it all. The most antagonism I faced, when working with those on the edges, came from some of the people who attended Mass each day and who did not like their Mass being attended, and sometimes interrupted, by those who had particular needs.

However, slowly, the Parish community was transformed by the very people some wanted to reject. Service of the poorest transforms us not them. More and more volunteers came to serve. Many more would come to the door with food and money, but what moved me most was the politeness and the laughter that eventually existed between those who served and those who came to be served. I often wondered who received the most benefit. I was moved by the generosity of many in the Parish community. We never ran out of money, food, clothes, or generous help from doctors, nurses, and chiropodists. We always found places for people in desperate need, and sometimes danger, to stay. The parish became one which was outward-looking, and which had loving compassionate service at its core. I thank God that I was part of it for so long.

I often wonder where Jesus would be found if he was physically amongst us. Maybe sitting in the shop doorways with those who live in that way. He might well be with those who have mental health issues and spend their days wandering around our town centres with little to help them. He would probably spend time with the young people who roam our estates and who have little value or future. We would find him with those who are excluded for whatever reason. Jesus would also be in the midst of the Scribes and Pharisees of our day challenging and encouraging us to change. If you want to become lively and vibrant and full of compassion and love, then serve the poorest of the poor and just see what happens.

Of course, there is a danger in thinking that the only people we are called to serve are the poor, those who are materially deprived. When Luke's Jesus stood up in the synagogue at Nazareth, he made it very clear that the call to serve was to all people. He chose the Sabbath when people gathered in the synagogue. Waiting to hear him would have been relatives, friends and neighbours as well as other people who lived there. He chose a passage from Isaiah to reveal that, in him, the prophets were to be fulfilled. He told them that the Spirit of the Lord had been given to him, as we saw in his baptism. Like the prophets in the Old Testament, he was anointed for mission to preach the Good News to the poor. But more than just that; he was to bring sight to the blind and liberty to captives. Who amongst us is not blind or bound up? The truth is that this message is not just for those out there but for you and me as well. What is it that holds us captive? What is it that binds us? What is the bitterness we cannot let go of, the secret relationship that has hurt us deeply, the anger we feel inside, the depression, the misery? What is it that holds us prisoner? Because this Gospel is for us if we only open our eyes and see? We carry around so much baggage that we do not need, and which stops us really experiencing the life that God invites us in to and so do others. Later on, Jesus gives examples of two Old Testament people who were helped by the Lord through his prophets. One was a poor widow and the other a rich man made poor by his illness. He finishes his inaugural address with the phrase that he has come, 'To set the downtrodden free and to proclaim the Lord's year of Favour'. This message is for every human being who has ever lived and who will ever live.

As I hope we have realised this Gospel is not just about personal relationship with the Lord, it also forces us into relationship with other people. The good news for the poor and the captives was that Jesus came to set them free. The blind, the captives, the, poor are all around us. They sit next to us on our public transport, in our restaurants, in our churches. They bump into us at the shops and walk past us in our high streets. We are called to serve the people of God and they come in many shapes and forms. It is to those who struggle to make sense of life and those appear not to that we have a mission with. It is to those people who appear to have it altogether and those who do not that we are invited to walk alongside. It is to those who have to bear the weight of prejudice and stigma for whatever reason, colour, creed, sexuality that we are called to love and accept. It is to those who are blind and yet cry out 'we see' that we are called.

I was once very blessed to meet Jimmy McGovern, the playwright. He is a very humble, self-effacing man who sees that he is called to highlight very difficult situations. It was my encounter with him that made me help to write a Lenten series around his programme 'Broken' that I mentioned earlier in this book. In Lent 2019 we ran this series in a fairly middle-class area. There were some people who got it immediately but there were others who felt that the scenes Jimmy and his scriptwriters had written did not really show modern Britain. They were shocked when I told them that the stories were all based on factual incidents. They could not believe that in Britain today those scenarios were a reality. I guess in order to serve, we have to open our eyes and really see. We have to put down our rose-tinted spectacles and see the world and its people as it is, and not as we want it to be. Anything else is a betrayal of the calling we are given, to live in our glorious messy world as servants of the Good News.

When Jesus finishes his address in the synagogue, he tells the people that this text was being fulfilled in him. Jesus makes it very clear that he does not share the mean image of God that the people of Nazareth have; that God is bigger, and God is more than they could even begin to imagine. So, he tells them that salvation is not just for the Jews, and it was too much for them to take. The immediate response is to cast doubt on what he is saying and to oppose him with violence. I guess we all do that when we hear something which makes us uncomfortable. We cast doubt on it until we do not have to believe it anymore and sometimes, we can be violent in our response. There is the challenge. Can we open our hearts to the message and the call without counting the cost?

Luke's Jesus invites us to walk with him in bringing life and salvation to our beautiful, yet fragile, world. I would like to finish this chapter with some words from Pope Francis on the feast of the Baptism of the Lord. He said, 'Our baptism has changed us, given us a new and glorious hope, and empowered us to bring God's redeeming love to all, particularly the poor, in whom we see the face of Christ. Our baptism has also given us a share in the church's mission of evangelisation; as disciples, we are also missionaries.'

TEN

LET MY PEOPLE GO

My uncle, Bob French, was a chief superintendent in special branch. He was a hard but fair man whose life was spent trying to protect those around him. As a child I was very scared of him. He seemed to be intransigent and insensitive. Probably because of his job, he always seemed to be watching and looking. He never talked about his work because he dealt with very sensitive issues. Despite all this, he was a good man, a man of faith, honesty, and integrity but a man who was cynical about people and what they were capable of. He used to laugh at my mum, his sister, because of her innate belief in the goodness of humanity. As I grew older and my fears were lessened, I began to appreciate uncle Bob and his desire to protect society and keep people safe.

One night, my brother Paul was bundled into a police van on his way home from his girlfriend's house. He was taken to the Police station and questioned about a series of robberies. Paul made one phone call from the police station and it was to Uncle Bob. Uncle Bob asked him one question, 'Are you guilty?' Paul said, 'No', and uncle Bob put the phone down. Paul said to me that the Police were being really difficult with him. They were on the point of charging him without any evidence, other than a possible identification, when the door of the interview room was thrown open and there stood Uncle Bob. Apparently the two policemen who were interviewing Paul went white. Uncle Bob very calmly walked across to the table, looked at the two policemen and said very quietly, 'Let my nephew go.' Then, he hammered on the table and shouted at the two men, 'Never try and stitch an innocent man up again.' With that, he took Paul by the arm and led him out of the room and out of the station. Needless to say, there were no charges brought. I remembered that incident when I sat down to write this chapter because, for me, in many senses, uncle Bob was like a type of Moses, with his command to let Paul go, echoing Moses' invitation to Pharaoh, to let the people of Israel go from captivity in Egypt.

At the beginning of Matthew's Gospel, in what we call the Infancy Narratives, we have Jesus presented to us as the new Moses. We all know the story of Moses and his murder of the Egyptian slave master. This led him to find himself at the bottom of the heap. He was a murderer on the run, caring for his father-in-law's sheep, living his life in fear. He has an extraordinary encounter with God in the burning bush, a bush that 'burns' without being consumed by the fire. This encounter with God leads Moses to know that the almighty God has visited him, and that he stands on holy ground. It is then, in the midst of this amazing experience, that he hears God's call on his life: 'I have heard the groaning of my people in Egypt. You, Moses, are to go confront the Pharaoh and tell him to let my people go.' (Exodus 3:9-10).

Richard Rohr says, 'There is no authentic God experience that does not situate you in the world in a different way. You see things differently, and you have the security to be free from your usual loyalties: privilege, position, group, and economy.' Moses has to face the consequences of being the agent of God's liberation and it costs him everything. Jesus as the new Moses will pay a similar cost for the liberation of God's people.

Megan McKenna in her book, 'Matthew: The Book of Mercy' writes, 'From the beginning of the Scriptures, God is the saviour of his people, liberating them from Egypt, from bondage, from their own weakness and betrayals, their lack of faithfulness to the covenant, bringing them back from the Exile and slavery, giving them the hope and the promises of the prophets. Yahweh God is a saving God and in this child Jesus God will now save all. This is God's work.'

The stories surrounding the birth of Jesus are largely theology rather than strict chronological history. I remember many years ago, teaching a course on the infancy narratives. After spending some time hammering home the point that the infancy narratives were theology rather than history I moved on. After a few moments, a plaintive voice was heard to cry out with a great deal of pathos, 'So there was no ...donkey?' Then the woman looked up and saw everyone looking at her and said, 'Oh no, have I just said that out loud?' It is hard for us, at times, to recognise how and why the Scriptures were written. It involves a lot of letting go of our pre-conceived ideas to find a deeper truth. Matthew has a theological purpose in writing these stories. They are not an account of what happened but are designed to make us ask ourselves the question. 'Who is this Jesus?' Can we see in him as Megan McKenna says, '...the work of God?' Are we able to recognise God's saving liberating power in the person of Jesus and in all he does and says? Can we experience his freedom deep within our hearts and in our lives? That is the challenge that the Jesus Matthew reveals to us; gives each one of us.

The presentation of Jesus as the new Moses starts with the massacre of the innocents. Like many of the stories told of the origins of Jesus birth we have no historical record that this really happened. Something as major as this would surely have been recorded somewhere. The question for us to ask is, what is Matthew trying to tell us about Christ? He is trying to connect Jesus to the massacre of all the elder sons when Pharaoh let the people out of Egypt. So, for Matthew, Jesus is the new Moses, leading the people out of slavery to freedom. Matthew is giving us a theology of Christ so that we might understand the extraordinary invitation to be free that we are given. It is not a freedom to do what we want, but a freedom to do what we are called to do. The inner freedom to do what reality demands of you is the only real freedom worth having. I think it is always worth saying that to live in the freedom of the children of God will lead us into conflict with the systems of this world. Indeed, the example of Jesus will invite us to stand against anything which threatens to overwhelm people. It will mean that issues of justice cannot be overlooked, even issues of justice within the Church. That freedom will invite us into the ways of compassion and love and mercy and forgiveness. It will mean, like Jesus, our friends will be the despised and the rejected. I suppose we should not really embrace this freedom unless we are seriously willing to go to Calvary.

We will be misunderstood and laughed at and dismissed as crazy fools. Certainly, in the Western world, that is the Calvary we are to embrace. In other parts of the world, it can cost us our very lives. Having said that, we will begin to know life in the most vibrant, rich depth. We will begin to understand what lasts for ever and what freedom that will bring.

A Jew who understood the Old Testament would immediately make the connections that Matthew is inviting us to make. Jesus is to be the new son coming out of Egypt into the Promised Land. Of course, Matthew has to find a way for Jesus to be the new Moses and lead the people out of Egypt, so he has to get him down to Egypt. Therefore, Mary and Joseph go down, across the Negev desert into Egypt. If you look at a map, or if you have been to the Holy Land, you would know that it is probably a physical impossibility for a woman on a donkey to undertake that journey. It is largely theology and it says something powerful about this Jesus.

In Jesus we find the whole of the Exodus story captured. He is the means to real freedom, and the way to experience God's desire for us. It is a hard-won freedom as Jesus will, in his own body, live out the pain and the struggle that the people went through when they were sent into exile. So, we have the Exodus and the exile summed up in the second part of the second chapter of Matthew's Gospel.

God went to extreme lengths to save Moses and now God is going to do the same thing to save Jesus. We are told that Joseph got up and took Jesus and his mother with him and went back to the land of Israel. These chapters are loaded with allusions to Jesus being the new Moses, who will give a new law to the people of God. That new law can be found later in the Gospel, in the Beatitudes which I have written about on many occasions.

To understand Matthew's presentation of Jesus it would be interesting to look at the way in which Matthew presents John the Baptist's teaching. In chapter three verse two, at the beginning of the book, we have a summary of John's teaching: 'Repent, for the kingdom of heaven is close at hand'. The Greek word that we translate as repent is metanoia, a word which is central to understanding the Gospel and which I have written about in several of my books and in previous chapters of this book.

There is a sense in which it could be said that, in its simplest form, metanoia means to turn around. The good news of the Gospel is that we are forgiven in Christ, so the challenge is to turn towards the light of forgiveness. Recently I listened to a woman tell me how her sister had hurt her very badly by not telling her that her mother had died. There was a huge amount of pain in what she shared, a catalogue of disasters that had led to this point. The woman said, after her initial response, she decided to bring forgiveness into the situation rather than continue the cycle of violence and be eaten up with anger and bitterness. Turn towards the light of forgiveness.

It is central to understanding the new, or second, testament to realise that we do not have to earn love. It is simply poured out upon us. The invitation is to turn towards love and let it flow through us healing, transforming, and freeing. Just recently at our sing-along for people living with dementia and their carers, I got into a conversation with a man who now looks after his mother. He told me that he had distanced himself from her when she was first diagnosed. He was unable to cope and the thought of what might happen was killing him inside. He was a nurse in a local hospital when he met an elderly man who came to have an ulcer on his leg dressed. It was a busy morning, and the man was in a hurry to be seen because he said that he had an appointment. The nurse said because the wound was healing well, he was able to redress the wound quite easily. During the conversation that ensued, the old man told him that his appointment was at a nursing home. He went there every day to eat breakfast with his wife. He said that she had been in the nursing home for a long time and was living with Alzheimer's Disease.

The man I was talking to was very professional but of course the conversation was becoming very difficult for him to handle. He finished dressing the man's wound and then he said that he asked if she would be worried if he was a bit late. The old man told my friend that his wife no longer knew who he was and had not recognised him in five years. I guess because he was thinking of his own situation and his mother who, at the time, he hardly saw, my friend blurted out, 'And you still go every morning, even though she does not know who you are?' Apparently, the old man smiled and patted my friend's hand and said, 'She does not know me, but I still know who she is.' The elderly man went on to say that he saw something similar on the internet and the phrase captured his situation beautifully and so he used it regularly when people asked why he went to his wife every morning. That encounter changed my friend's life and as soon as his shift finished, he went around to his mother's house and since then has spent his life looking after her. Turn towards the light of unconditional love.

To turn around and face the light, letting go of our need to control, takes us into another realm where it is God who does the transforming. My friend Nicki has a mental health issue, but she does not allow that to stop her knowing that she is a child of God with a unique dignity. That is not always easy for her but despite her issues she always looks to the light and tries to trust in God more than in herself. Just recently, she told me that she had not really liked sharing with others how intelligent she is. Before her illness took over her life, she had hoped to study medicine. Since her illness was diagnosed, she has covered up her intelligence and never acknowledged it. Recently, she has been attending a place called Life Rooms which is welcoming and open to all people but particularly those with mental health issues. Nicki has always loved music and in the past had some musical ability. She signed up for a course in classical music, but she thought people might reject her if they knew how talented she is. Her lack of honesty about this was upsetting her so she decided honesty was the best policy. So, during one of the sessions on the course, she told others the instruments she had played and how much music meant to her. Of course, no-one rejected her but what mattered to Nicki was that she had turned towards the light and believed the truth about herself and that had freed her.

We are all being called to realise our dignity and the freedom that brings. When in the process of transformation, we begin to know who we are - children of an unconditionally loving God. We begin to understand that our well-being is not dependent on what others think or whether we are at the centre of everything but on God and God alone. That is where transformation leads, and it will take us into a deep love for the world and for others.

A few months ago, I was with a woman I know very well who lives with schizophrenia. The drugs she is on control her condition really well but she still suffers from anxiety and at times is haunted by her past. She was describing what it was like when she was young and would become psychotic.

She talked about the fear that overwhelmed her and the panic that engulfed her so much that she would shake from head to foot and try and harm herself just to get relief. She talked of her mum who would come and wrap her arms around her and hold her till the shaking subsided even when the daughter was violent. I thought about the mother a lot after she had been talking to me. She was prepared to put herself in danger for the sake of her daughter. It was all for love and, in many senses, it is an image of the love of God for us and the mystery of a human soul so transformed that love becomes the only way.

All of that turning is summed up in the word metanoia. The process of metanoia is all about what God wants to do within us, not about what we want to do for God. When we allow it to happen within us it will change everything.

That is the freedom that Jesus came to bring, and it is all there in that little phrase, 'Repent for the kingdom of heaven is close at hand'. Biblical repentance has little to do with whipping ourselves for our sins. That is the misunderstanding. It has everything to do with seeing in a different way because of the work of God within us; that is the conversion. It is an invitation to change direction and enter into what Matthew calls the 'Kingdom of Heaven'. In trying to explain the value of the kingdom, Jesus tells us this parable: The Kingdom of God is like a merchant in search of fine pearls. When he finds a single one of great value, he goes and sells all that he owns and buys that pearl. Ronald Rolheiser, the Canadian oblate, when reflecting on the parable says, 'What is our own pearl of great price? Are we willing to give up everything in exchange for it?'

I think it would be fair to say when reading the Gospels that Jesus was never frustrated or sour that he had given his life for the sake of others. To live for the kingdom meant everything to him. Jesus always seemed to be gregarious and joyful. He was compassionate, loving, open free, forgiving and non-judgmental. His whole life was given away for others and it seemed to fulfil everything that he desired. It is all to do with finding that pearl of great price.

Many years ago, I met a man called John. He was in his mid 50's at the time. He was married with five children all crammed into a small two bedroomed terraced house and he exuded joy. His eyes were twinkling all the time and he was full of laughter. He was warm, compassionate and loving and he fascinated me because his life was really very ordinary and actually quite difficult. He did not have a lot of money or an abundance of material goods. He worked as a labourer on various building sites, and when he did not have any work, he and his family just about survived. We sat having a pint one night and he told me that, many years earlier, he had a very bad breakdown. His first wife had died at a very early age and life no longer seemed worth living. He tried to take his own life because he felt so lost and abandoned and it was when he was recovering in a psychiatric unit that a chaplain came to visit him. The chaplain listened to him over several weeks as John cried away his pain and heartache and then asked him if he could he pray for him. John agreed and as the man prayed, he said that he felt something shift within. He was flooded with a deep sense of joy and he realised that God was with him. He had found the pearl of great price and nothing had ever taken it away from him. There was a deep and lasting change that took place in his life, so much so that when I met him, his whole life was lived for the sake of the Gospel. Freedom and new life was his.

So, Matthew presents Jesus as the new Moses freeing us to live in the kingdom of God, freeing us to find the pearl of great price. As the Gospel unfolds, we find that Jesus concentrates totally on bringing freedom to God's people. He preaches the new law in the Beatitudes, a law written on our hearts, that brings deep inner freedom. Throughout the rest of the Gospel, we are going to discover that the freedom promised to us in him is lived out in the relationships that we have with one another. God's presence impinges on our lives through the way we treat one another.

So, Jesus says, do not judge and you will not be judged, do not condemn and you will not be condemned. Seek justice, and peace and gentleness. Be salt for the world and light to the nations. In so far as we are prepared to love one another, forgive one another, care for one another, then we are being led into the Promised Land of life and life in its fullness. As long as we refuse to do those things, we stay in slavery in the Egypt of our own making.

In his encounters with people, freedom is always the outcome for those who want to experience freedom, and not all of us do. I love the story of the Gadarene demoniacs that we find in chapter 8 which symbolises the freedom that we are called to. Two men lived possessed by demons. Jesus confronts the demons and sends them into the herd of pigs that were grazing nearby. Not even the pigs wanted the demons that were in the men to be in them, and so they rushed over the edge of the cliff. The men were free, but sometimes freedom can be scary. When the people saw the demoniacs in their full senses, they begged Jesus to leave. Often, we seem to want religion with all its trappings but not always the freedom that God wants to bring. He makes it very clear in his exchanges with the Scribes and Pharisees, those who think they are free, that they are not free at all but bound by religion.

Many years ago, I met Leonardo Boff, the great Brazilian liberation theologian. He was visiting Cafod in England and I was lucky enough to spend some time listening to him. Liberation theology, which grew from the heart of the poor in South America, has had its critics down the years, but it seems to me that the Exodus story is liberation theology in every way but name. Jesus, as the new Moses, fully captures what is at the heart of liberation theology. It is obvious from the Gospels that Jesus is on the side of the little ones and is a healer of the poor and powerless.

However, liberation theology focuses on freeing people from more than just their personal burdens. It focuses of systemic sin too. Religious, political, social, and economic oppression are all drawn under the spotlight. So, it goes beyond just trying to free individuals from their own weakness and vulnerability, which many people identify as the only meaning of sin and looks towards the wider understanding. Just as Moses threatened the system that kept people in slavery in the Exodus story, so too, when Jesus challenged the Scribes and the Pharisees, he was threatening the whole Judaic system. I often think to myself, it is no wonder that Jesus was killed. Marcus Borg who is a New Testament scholar, writes, 'The way of Jesus was both personal and political. It was about personal transformation and it was political. It was a path of [nonviolent] resistance to the domination system and advocacy of an alternative vision of life together under God. His counter advocacy, his passion for God's passion, led to his execution.'

We human beings always want to kill that which threatens our security. In a more, supposedly advanced, culture we no longer do it by crucifying those who threaten us, but we take away their good name. We imprison them through the cult of the media. We ridicule them and call them dreamers. As Richard Rohr often says, Jesus would be crucified today, but just in a different way, and maybe even by the Church.

So, Jesus is presented by Matthew as the new Moses setting his people free from any kind of slavery both personal and institutional. He is the one who leads us to freedom if we allow him the space to do that. It is a freedom which is spacious and bountiful, in which we discover what it means to be human and alive, in which we discover what we are meant to be, and which leads us to life in its fullness.

ELEVEN

Freedom and Mercy go Hand in Hand

The man was dying of aids. He had never told any of his friends that he was gay. It was his secret. When they knew what was causing his cough and why he had lost so much weight, one by one, they abandoned him. Full of bitterness and anger, he hid himself away awaiting his fate. He grew weaker and weaker as time went on. Some days he was scarcely able to drag himself from his bed, the pain in his body was so great and the exhaustion he felt so powerful.

One day his door-bell rang. The district nurse who dealt with his medication in her cool calm way, had left and so the man went slowly and painfully to the door. Standing on the step was a man who told him he was from the local Church and asked if he could come in. At first there was reluctance but eventually the two men found themselves sitting drinking tea.

'I'm dying of aids,' he blurted out. 'I know' said the man from the Church with tears in his eyes. He stood up and went to the other man and held his thin emaciated body as it began to wrack with tears.

When the tears stopped, and the two men were sitting again, the one who was dying said to the other, 'I want to meet your God when I die'. The other looked puzzled, 'What do you mean?' he said. The aids sufferer looked into the other's eyes. 'You drank from my cup,' he said, 'even though you knew what was wrong with me. Your eyes filled with tears when I cried. You held me. You accepted me. Your God is the God I want to meet when I die.' One man who was free enough and merciful enough to show the face of Christ to the other. The coming together of freedom and mercy. In the last chapter we reflected on the freedom that is in the heart of God for us. The face of Christ that is revealed by Matthew is all about Jesus as the new Moses calling us to that extraordinary freedom that is the desire of God for us.

Megan McKenna, as I mentioned in the last chapter, has written a fantastic book called 'Matthew: The Book of Mercy' and in it she says, 'Mercy is the ink, the paper, the background, the words and the meaning, in and through, and under everything. Everything that Jesus says and does, his very presence and his coming upon earth is mercy.' I have no doubt that freedom and mercy go hand in hand. We both have to know, and experience, mercy if we are to receive and show mercy. So, yes, the Jesus that Matthew reveals is the new Moses, but he is also revealed, in the Gospel, as the face of God's mercy. Again, it is McKenna who writes, 'God is the God of mercy. Mercy is made real in the practice of forgiveness, reconciliation and atonement, meaning at-one-ment and restoration, meaning to repair the broken pieces.' All of that we see in Matthew's Jesus and it is those realities I would like to explore in this chapter to deepen our awareness of Matthew's Jesus.

Mercy is made real in the act of forgiveness. Throughout what we call the sermon on the mount in chapters five to seven, Jesus challenges us to move deeply into the whole area of merciful forgiveness. Matthew has Jesus remind us to love our enemies. That call to forgiveness must be the most radical call on our lives. Love those who hurt you. It is almost impossible.

Ronald Rolheiser, the Canadian oblate, writes, 'Can you love an enemy? can you truly forgive someone who has hurt you? can you bless someone who has cursed you? can you be good to those who have done you harm? can you forgive a murderer? This challenge is what sets Jesus' moral teaching apart from others and gives it its unique character - and its real teeth. This is meant to be the distinguishing mark of a follower of Jesus: he or she can love and forgive an enemy.'

I think that can only be done in the power of God and when we are aware of our own need for mercy. Are you known for the forgiveness that lies in your heart? Are you seen to be someone who is always leading the way in that area of forgiveness? What's your reaction to those who hurt you or hurt those close to you? What about those who commit atrocities against the whole of society?

As the sermon gathers pace, we are invited to pray for forgiveness in the 'Our Father'. Forgiveness is the greatest sign of the Kingdom of God which is at the heart of Matthew's Gospel. I often think that the 'Our Father' is really a very simple prayer focusing on God and God's providence. However, like most simple realities, it has a sting in the tail when it reminds us that if we pray it, our words and deeds have to reflect one another. 'Forgive us our trespasses as we forgive those who trespass against us.' One of the keys to understanding how to forgive, is relationship. In the Lord's Prayer we are invited to enter into a whole new way of relating to God. The invitation is to relate to God as Jesus does. It is to know God as Abba. It is to radically re-think our understanding of God. God who, for most of the ancient peoples, has been distant, scary and unapproachable becomes warm, close and relatable to. I think I only really understood the word Abba when I was staying in Jerusalem with my friend George. He left me one day with his little boy Rafi while he went to the shops. Rafi and I were watching Spiderman. George came through the door with his arms full of bags and Rafi who was about six at the time hurled himself at his dad shouting 'Abba' over and over. He threw his arms around his dad and clung to him saying, 'Abba, Abba.' When we really know God as Abba, the chasm of love opens wide and we are drawn into it and then it flows from us. It is a huge turning around that we are called to if we are to be a people of forgiving mercy. It is in that relationship that we pray for the coming of the Kingdom when everyone will know that God is enough and our fruitless searching for fulfilment will be over and forgiveness will flow freely.

Forgiveness rises to the fore again in chapter seven when Matthew has Jesus say, 'Do not judge'. It is so easy to fall into the trap of being harsh and judgemental. All that does is destroy humanity. When we refuse to allow people to escape from what they have done or what we think they have done, we bind them, and they cannot experience freedom. It is why Matthew reflects so much on judgement and sees non-judgement as the cornerstone for a healthy society.

I suppose it is all captured in the one sentence, 'Treat others as you would have them treat you'. Biblical scholars call it the golden rule. It is another way of saying, 'Love your neighbour as yourself.' Right at the heart of that truth is the power of forgiving mercy. When we move further on in the Gospel, we discover, in chapter 18, a reflection on how we are to live. We are to be the 'little ones,' and our main characteristic is to be forgiveness. You will find the story of the lost sheep and the parable of the unforgiving servant as well as the way to deal with those who sin against the community. It is constant forgiveness and mercy and compassion. I think it is a lesson we have still to learn in a Church which prides itself on power and authority and control. We are so far from the concept of the little ones it is unbelievable, and we have to ask the question what role forgiveness plays, not just in our own lives, but in the life of the institution.

A few years ago, I met a librarian in a retreat centre. We had many interesting conversations. John had a very tough life. His mother was alcoholic, and John hardly ever went to school. He spent most of his time trying to look after his mother. When he was seven, he was taken into care and placed in an orphanage, where he was not treated well or kindly by the staff and the nuns who looked after him. As he shared his story, I heard of situations that were abusive and cruel. I listened as he bravely talked of battling against bullying in school and triumphing through his natural intelligence. He had eventually gone to University where he had done well and was now married with three children, who he adored. What amazed me was the depth of forgiveness in his heart for the people who had hurt him. What amazed me was that there was not a trace of rancour or bitterness within him, simply loving forgiveness. He said that he had found that way many years earlier when he had cried out to God because he was drowning in hatred of those who had hurt him and he realised that in order to be free, he had to forgive. God heard his prayer and he found the strength over a period of time to forgive and let go and find peace. So, Matthew shows us the face of God's mercy though forgiveness.

Mercy is made real in the act of reconciliation. Reconciliation is the coming together of that which is out of balance. It is the drawing together and making whole of what is apart or broken. The human race needs reconciliation. We need to be reconciled within ourselves. We are all very broken people and I think we are all fragmented inside. We all do the things we do not want to do, and we do not do the things we want to do. We are torn apart inside by insecurities and jealousies and fears and anxieties.

We need to be reconciled with God. God is closer to us than the very air that we breathe and yet, too often, we go it alone, somehow thinking we are in control. As a race, we do not trust God. Most people do not even believe in God. We need to be reconciled with one another. We all have relationships that have gone wrong. We have all fallen out with people. We all take instant dislikes to people for no good reason. Most of us have misunderstood people and judged them and condemned them. We need to be reconciled with the world. Even if we do not particularly do anything ourselves, we are all caught up in systems that are unjust, and we support them even by default.

So, Matthew's Jesus will preach reconciliation to show the mercy of God by what he does and what he says. He will heal the centurion's servant, breaking down the barriers we put up against one another. He will bring life to lepers and those who need healing. He will tell parables about the kingdom and in them all he is drawing the people of God together, into a new way of living. If you look at the Gospel of Matthew, Jesus does not teach us how to be virtuous or how to be saved, even how to be a good church-goer. He says little or nothing about knowing dogma or following a strict moral code. Instead he simply heals and reconciles.

In chapter 19, Jesus reflects on relationships and on reconciliation, the drawing together of that which is broken as a facet of mercy. After his teaching on divorce, Matthew focuses on the Kingdom and the need to draw together the people of God if the Kingdom is to be seen to be real. He writes, 'Let the little children alone and do not stop them coming to me'. Matthew reminds us that it is the little ones, the powerless ones, who understand the Kingdom. What is Matthew saying to us? That if we want to experience the kingdom we have to become like little children. We have to let go of our blindness, which is caused by the pain and hurt that many of us go through. We have to let go of the walls of cynicism and bitterness that we build up to protect ourselves and be reconciled.

Almost to illustrate the point, in verses 16-22 we have the story of the rich young man who wants to know what he must do to have eternal life. It is interesting to note that for him, it is all about what he can do, when the truth is it is about what God can do; and in Jesus what God can do is pour out mercy as he invites the rich young man to be reconciled to his community by giving what he has to the poor. The focus is always on God for the disciple. It was not wrong for the rich young man to have his possessions, but they had become his focus and only God should have that place. When the young man persists, Jesus goes to the heart of the matter. 'Sell what you have....' What is it that blocks the flow of mercy in your life? What is it that stops you receiving mercy and letting mercy flow into the lives of others? It has to be the unwillingness to stand alongside the poor and the broken. The young man went off sad because he had great possessions. They possessed him, they blocked the flow of mercy and they blocked relationship. He had to let go to follow Jesus. What Jesus asks the young man to do, he is asking of all of us; to be aware of what possesses us and let go. There is a wonderful line in the story where Jesus looks at the young man and loves him. Mercy flows from one to the other but the young man has to be open to it, as we all do.

Matthew then reflects on the 'treasure' that is ours if we turn around and let go of all that shackles us and begin to live in the kingdom of mercy. Entry into the Kingdom cannot be bought, earned or conquered. We can gain the whole world, win the lottery and yet lose ourselves. The Kingdom is about finding our true selves and letting mercy and justice, God's justice, flow into the world. Peter then has to have his say. He and the others have left everything to follow Jesus. That ought to be worth something! They have missed the point again. It is not about what they get out of it but about what God wants to give. It is mercy and justice overflowing from the heart of God. We so often miss the point. We try to buy our way into heaven by the number of times we go to Mass, or the novenas we say, or by keeping the commandments; but it is not about any of that. It is simply about letting God love us and restore us, so that we can recognise the Kingdom and share the kingdom. Stop trying to get to heaven and let God get heaven into you.

The parable of the vineyard labourers obviously pre-dates the trade union movement! It really gets on our craw. Once again, mercy is at the heart of this story, mercy that is for all people everywhere and at any time. Matthew wants us to understand that in the eyes of God, all people are equal, that Jews and Gentiles are seen as equals in the Kingdom. God is the giver and pours out healing and reconciliation on all of us equally.

I have written about my great aunt Lizzie before. She lived in Bootle in a big house which had servants' quarters, and she fell out with the rest of her family for a variety of reasons. Her husband, John Sloan Barclay, had been married before and he brought two sons from his first marriage. He was quite well off and ran his own business, hence the big house in Bootle with servants' quarters. He and Lizzie had five daughters before John sadly died, leaving Lizzie to bring up the five girls. The two sons who were much older had already left home. John, I am told, was a mason and the masons were very good to his family, making sure that there was money available to support the boys in what they were doing and money to educate the girls. So Lizzie was quite well off and able to bring up her children as she would have wanted to. By the time the girls were adults, several of them had seemingly developed mental health issues. They were very difficult, and the family home was often full of tension. I was told by a neighbour that the fighting and the rows between the girls was legendary and on more than one occasion one or other of them had to be carted off to an institution. As the years went by, they all fell out with each other until no-one was speaking. The eldest, Hilda, stayed at home with her mother, looking after the house. Doris, who was next, joined the Queen Alexandra nurses and settled in Australia as far away as she could. Muriel was, at times in her life, very ill and died in an institution. There were twins who followed. Lilian was also very ill and died in a bedsit in Southport surrounded by newspapers. Edna spent most of her life on lithium and ended up, after three husbands, living in a remote part of New Zealand. There was so much mercy and reconciliation needed in that family and very sadly it never happened until the day that the youngest daughter, Edna, returned to Liverpool. She visited the graves of her sisters and her parents and made peace with them. She lived the rest of her life freed from the pain of her background and grateful for God's mercy.

Mercy is made real through atonement or at-one-ment. This is best seen in Matthew's reflection on the death of Jesus, where Jesus draws together every strand of brokenness and pain that has ever been and transforms it into new life. He becomes at one with the whole of humanity in its need for real deep reconciliation and harmony. I have often written that the largely unhelpful theology of substitution, that is Jesus taking our place on the cross, has, at its worst, led us to see God as a distant, cold, angry, brutal figure. This God demands vengeance for our sins through the violent taking of life before God can ever love humanity and the world. Richard Rohr writes, 'The theory of substitutionary atonement has inoculated us against the true effects of the Gospel, causing us to largely 'thank' Jesus instead of honestly imitating him.'

In both the first and second testament there are metaphors of sacrifice, ransom, atonement, paying the price, and opening the gates that would have made sense to the ordinary Jew. Sadly, they seem to tell us that God is not fundamentally on our side. Those sorts of images mean we have to find a way of appeasing God and making God love us. We do that through believing certain formulae and saying the right words, getting the ritual right, so that God will favour us.

Any contemporary reading of the Scriptures will always pull you towards looking for meaning. I think when we read the Scriptures with both our brains and our hearts switched on, we begin to recognise that what we have is a faith story of the people of God. At times this means the words they used, even the theology they used, was growing and developing. Sometimes the language, metaphors and images have lost their meaning in the realms of time and culture. Jesus' death on the cross was a visual image of what God has always been, even when people did not quite understand. God has always been love, mercy, forgiveness, and reconciliation, always! Jesus captures that on the cross so that we might see it for all time and know the truth that we are forgiven and loved and cherished. We always have been and always will be.

Again, it is Rohr who says, 'As long as we employ any retributive notion of God's offended justice (required punishment for wrongdoing), we trade our distinctive Christian message for the cold, hard justice that has prevailed in many cultures throughout history. We offer no redemptive alternative, but actually sanctify the very 'powers and principalities' that Paul says unduly control the world (Ephesians 3:9-10; 6:12).' That means we never understand the bigger picture of who God is and who we are. We somehow get locked into a small, narrow understanding where God is far less than God is and simply wants to punish a bad and errant world. Matthew's Jesus hangs on the cross to draw together broken humanity. He hangs on the cross to be at one with humanity that often feels abandoned and alone He hangs on the cross to be a sign of unity drawing all things together. He hangs there as the eternal icon of God's reconciling mercy.

I remember preaching about this many years ago and at the end a man came up to me with tears pouring down his face. He told me that he had been brought up a Catholic and for a variety of reasons had left the Church. Some years earlier his mother had died, and that experience had brought him back. However, he said that he had struggled to understand why Jesus had to die, and each Good Friday he would never go to Church because he couldn't handle the image that he was given; and yet he knew that the cross was vital and at the centre of faith. His issue was that he could not equate a loving merciful God, with the God who sent Jesus to die on a cross, and rather than be faced with the issue, he stayed away. As I preached about the cross, he found himself crying and saying to Jesus, 'So that is who you are, that is what it is about'.

Mercy is made real through restoration. Throughout the Gospel, Jesus is presented as the one who moves beyond any teaching that is retributive. So, in the sermon on the mount, we will find Jesus teaching his disciples to move beyond even equitable retribution and saying, turn the other cheek if someone strikes you. If anyone would take your coat, give your cloak as well. If you are forced to go one mile with someone, go two. It is the face of mercy being shown and it is all about the restorative justice that was mentioned in an earlier chapter. This sort of justice which is in God, is about rehabilitation, healing, and reconciliation. It is never about punishment. Restorative justice is seen most clearly in the healing ministry of Jesus.

Many years ago, I met a man who taught me the truth of restoration, rather than retribution. His son had gone into the city centre and never returned. He had been murdered because someone was jealous of his new training shoes. The young man who had stabbed him was tried and sent to prison for life. This father did not seek retribution. Indeed, he went one stage further. He went to the prison and saw his son's murderer and forgave him in the hope that forgiveness would enable his son's murderer to turn his life around. Restoration rather than retribution is the face of mercy.

Throughout the Gospel, as was said earlier, Matthew presents Jesus as the one who heals and restores. This image of the merciful face of God is the one that Matthew wants us to know most fully. Even the challenges Jesus gave, chiefly to the Scribes and the Pharisees, were always to enable people to move into the areas of healing and restoration. So, Matthew's Jesus is merciful, and his mercy enables us to experience freedom, the sort of freedom that allows us to be who we are called to be and to do what is really demanded of us for the sake of the world.

TWELVE

FREED TO LIVE

E very time I take a group to the Holy Land, I always try to give them some time off. It can be a very intense experience because it seems to be one of those 'thin places' that the ancient Celts talked about, places where the presence of God is almost tangible. So, a bit of space can really help people process what is happening inside them. I usually spend my time off in Jerusalem, wandering around the old city. I love the atmosphere, the colour and the vibrancy of the place. On one occasion, recently, I was doing just that. I was in the Moslem quarter of the old city with a couple of friends, drinking in the atmosphere and maybe not taking as much care as I should about where I was walking. The streets are narrow, cobbled and crowded. To this day I do not know what happened, but I found myself beginning to fall and after a few moments of what seemed like slow motion I hit the ground, with a great deal of force, face downwards.

For a moment I was stunned. It was as though all the air had been squeezed out of my body and then as I drew breath, I could taste the blood in my mouth and for a moment I thought, 'Oh no, my teeth have shattered, or I have broken my nose.' The person I had been walking with got a real fright and immediately ran some distance. He told me afterwards he thought I had been shot! Since then I have re-named him 'Peter'! The others I was with, were some distance back and it took them a while to catch up. So,

I lay on the floor unable to move with no-one helping me, when several Moslems ran over to me and to my shame, I was anxious, wondering what they might do to me. I kept trying to push them away saying, through the blood and mucus, that I was fine. It was really because of fear of the unknown. One of them spoke in perfect English. He told me that he was a doctor from Derby, visiting his parents who lived and worked in the old city. He was a beautiful man, full of gentleness and kindness. He helped me to sit up and examined me then he washed my face and gave me water to drink, telling me that nothing was broken, I was just bruised and that all the blood was from a cut on my lip. Despite my shame, I was immensely grateful to him and his friends.

I realised when I was back in the hotel just how much freedom I need in my life. I have always considered myself to be open and accepting of others but that day, in my vulnerability, all my hidden prejudices rose to the surface. I now know how much freedom I really need to experience, particularly freedom from prejudice and fear. Thank God, that is God's desire for me too. God wants us all to be healed and free because of that extraordinary love that God has for us. Heidi Baker, who is a well-known evangelical preacher, wrote this, 'God's love is big enough to touch any life, to make light out of any darkness. Jesus came that we might have life, so that no more would we have to die in depression, anger or pain. He loved people back to life. He would go anywhere, talk to anyone and wherever he went, he would stop for the one – the forgotten one, the one who was rejected, outcast, sick, even stone dead. Even a thief who was dying for his crimes on the cross next to him. In the kingdom of

God's love there is no one who cannot come home.' I guess that indicates that we are loved and cherished by God in a way that goes beyond our wildest concepts and images of God. It is so difficult to put words on the nature and truth of God's love. Whatever inadequate words we use to try and express God's love, I think it is true to say that God does not want us to be tied up in the mess of our lives but to be free to really live.

Richard Rohr, says, 'A good spirituality achieves two huge things simultaneously: It keeps God absolutely free, not bound by any of our formulas, and it keeps us utterly free ourselves, not forced or constrained by any circumstances. When these two great freedoms meet, we have a spiritual awakening. And the world opens up beneath our feet and above our heads. We are in a differently shaped universe.' The freedom that Jesus offers is something we grow into. It does not usually happen overnight. It is to enter into the arena of the movement, and action of the Spirit. It is when we are slowly freed from the self, from the concerns of the ego, from our own obsessions and neurotic behaviour, from our own need to be significant to ourselves or others. It is, of course, a freedom, from that which keeps us bound, and sadly, many of us do not recognise that we are bound. It is the freedom to be who we are and do what we are called to do. That sort of freedom is always the work of the Spirit and is always a gift. I wonder why we fight against it so much. Could it be that it is too demanding to be really and truly free?

Just recently, I was in Northumberland, walking up to Cuthbert's cave, an over-hanging outcrop of Sandstone rock, supported by an isolated pillar of stone. Tradition holds that, in AD 875, the monks of Lindisfarne walked across the causeway and brought St. Cuthbert's body to this place to rest for a short period following Viking raids on Holy Island. It is a beautiful place, and as I walked in the sunshine with the wind on my face, I felt an incredible freedom deep inside myself. Eventually I reached the cave and some of the group I was with settled there, but the rest of us carried on to the pinnacle above the cave where we could see Holy Island in the distance. I was trying to reflect on why I felt so free in that place and I realised it was because while I was there, I had nothing to protect, nothing to control and no-one to impress. I had a sense of the presence of God and the wonder of my own being. It was fantastic. I realised afterwards of course that the freedom to be who I truly am is always costly. It is not always easy to be free and to live in today's society with the demands that are placed upon us. It is with great difficulty that we try to live untrammelled by the expectations of others. It can be hard to be comfortable in our own skin and yet open enough to embrace and welcome everyone and anyone. It is difficult to learn how to give yourself away for the sake of others and yet that is the freedom that Christ came to bring us.

If you read St Paul's letters, he tells us that the question of freedom is all about the false self and the true self. He talks of spirit and flesh. He sees flesh as the false self and spirit as the true self. I know that I have written more fully about this in other books, but for our purposes in this chapter, it would be worth reflecting for a short while again. The false self is the one that tries to stay in control of life, the future and others. It focuses entirely on what is good for me and leads inevitably to our being fragile, needy, and insecure. The false self is the source of much of the blame and scapegoating which dogs our culture. It is a very limiting reality in which our world becomes narrow and small. It is so sad to see most of humanity living in this way, in this tiny little self that needs so much affirmation and praise.

The true self is who we really are in God. It offers us the chance to live a life that has broad horizons. It is a way of life that is spacious and open in which nothing is rejected but everything is held and acknowledged. It comes about through that spiritual awakening, which is the gift of the Spirit. It is that sudden understanding of who we are in God's sight and knowing the truth that we are beloved. It is recognising with gratitude that God holds our very existence in the palm of God's hands and that we can fall into limitless grace. The call to freedom is to journey from the narrow, limited experience of the false self to the open, whole, warm experience of the true self. That is what the biblical understanding of transformation is all about and until we begin to let the Spirit lead us in that way, we have not begun to taste the freedom that is in the heart of God for us.

John Beirne was my mum's closest friend. He was a priest in the archdiocese of Liverpool and was one of the most influential priests on my own journey to priesthood. He was a very warm, open, human person. There was no guile in him and he never seemed to worry or be anxious about life. He had a great sense of humour and was good company to be with. John always had time for people. When speaking to him it was as though one was the only person in the world. I never saw him lose his temper or try to avoid difficult people. He seemed to understand humanity. He lived and worked for many years in a small village church and was known and loved by everyone there. God was at the centre of his life in a simple, non-threatening way. He loved God with everything that he was. He told me once that he left Wigan to train in Lisbon as a young boy, wet behind the ears, and returned a priest. He said that he was still wet behind the ears but as a priest in the 1940's the culture was such that your own vulnerability was never mentioned. He said that the experience of not being with or seeing his family damaged him quite badly. As the years went on, he realised that in order to be free he had to let go, not only of the hurt but also of the certainties and the clericalism that he had been brought up with, and to some degree trained in. It was a long hard journey, as it is for all of us, but John found his true self in God and lived most of his life as a truly warm, open, loving human being and I thank God for him regularly because, without even knowing it, he was a great influence on me, just by being.

To enter into the freedom that is in the heart of God for us calls for a lot of letting go. It demands that we let go of false images of God and ourselves. It invites us to face that which keeps us trapped in the small self. I think the Gospel invites us to face our own pain and the hurts that we cover up, but which dominate and control us from a place deep within. This often leads us to live as stunted human beings. That call to deep freedom invites us to realise we are not in control of our own lives. It frees us to love and that is frightening because it is costly. There is a song that we sometimes sing in our community and one of the verses based on Galatians 5, says, 'It was for freedom that Christ has set us free.' True freedom does not mean that you can do what you want to do. It means you are free to do what God wants you to, to find the inner detachment, the inner freedom to live the Gospel for others. We are being invited to be the presence of God in the world. It means that we are to be love for the world, to be forgiveness for the world, to be peace makers in the world, to be accepting and non-judgemental. That is where transformation is leading us and that is real freedom. I suppose that is the reason why over the last couple of years, Pope Francis has been talking a lot about untying the knots in our lives and finding freedom. He wants a Church that is outward looking, rather than one which is self-serving. He wants a Church that is free to proclaim the good news of God's love and which can get dirty, broken, and bruised on the way. The question for us is whether we want to give our lives to that reality or not? Do we want to build a Church based on relationship and all that means - relationship with the Lord and with one another empowered by the Spirit or do we want to continue to build up a structure that is weighed down by the scourge of clericalism, and power and authoritarianism. My sense is that a Church built on those things will ultimately collapse and maybe that is what we are beginning to see. However, a Church built on the power of faith in Christ and one another can never be overcome. A Church that is a servant seeking only to love, forgive and let compassion reign will last until the end of time. Let's have the courage to open ourselves to the Lord and build that Church. To live as that sort of Church we have to be free and Matthew's Jesus certainly wants us to experience that freedom.

So how do we enter into the process of letting go in order to find freedom? I suppose it demands a certain honesty. What is it that we hold on to and seem unable to let go of? What knots have we tied ourselves up in that make us bitter and angry? What hurts keep returning to haunt us? How can we let go? These are the sort of questions we are to reflect on if we are to experience the freedom that God wants for us.

Many years ago, I came across a man whose life had been tragically marred by his childhood experiences. He was so badly damaged that much of his way of thinking, particularly about himself, was twisted and broken. Three marriages and several other failed relationships had not helped the situation. Yet he was one of the warmest, kindest people you could meet. In time his desperate search for love and acceptance led him to our community. We became good friends, but he struggled to believe the things that he heard and saw, and I spent many hours listening to, and praying for, him.

Trusting that people were on his side and that God was on his side was the most difficult area for him to cope with. There were times of absence when he just could not cope and would stay away from us; and there were times of deep depression as his memories tortured him. It was while we were at a healing service that he was cured of arthritis in his knees, but decided it was all psychosomatic. It had nothing to do with the goodness of God and so the battle went on for many years. Then he was diagnosed with an aggressive and rare cancer and something, I think the action of the Spirit, happened within him. The healing that he had always desired began to take place. He was transformed within as the cancer ravaged his body. He began to know that he was loved by God and by those around him. He forgave people who had damaged him so badly and he learned how to trust. As he went through treatment after treatment, he was like a light as he shared with others the presence of the God that he knew was with him and who loved him. He eventually died aged 64, a healed, whole, free man, finally at peace.

I think it would be fair to say that most human beings are very badly damaged for all sorts of reasons. We are damaged by our parents, our siblings, our teachers, our friends, the Church and many other groups. If that is the case, then we need to face our inner condition in order to find peace and freedom. In Matthew and Dennis Linn's book, 'Healing Life's Hurts', the authors remind us that there is no time in God. They express a truth that I have certainly discovered in my own life. It is this: if we believe that Jesus is alive, then we can ask the Lord to walk back in time to the moment or the period of time when we were hurt and free us from the effects of that wound in the present. We can ask the Lord to heal, now, the effects and wounds within me and within the other person or people involved.

Of course, as I have said, this involves bringing to light the things that have hurt us. It is the most difficult thing to do because that hurt can be so painful but not to do it can make it worse. J.K. Rowling in Harry Potter and the Goblet of Fire wrote, 'Numbing the pain for a while will make it worse when you finally feel it.' It is almost always worth talking the pain through with someone else because the talking out of the problem is, in itself, part of the healing process. There is a danger in this, that it can be self-indulgent, but it is never self-indulgent if the whole point of sharing the pain is to find a new way of living. Never ever rule out professional help. It can be extraordinarily beneficial to have help from someone who has the skills to really help you unlock your pain. It can be a way of showing that you are committed to growth as a person. I know that for me, counselling was the most freeing, liberating experience and really helped me in the process of letting go.

Henri Nouwen, the great spiritual writer, had some very wise advice in this whole area. Writing in his journal during a time of bitter heartbreak, he wrote these words: 'The great challenge is living your wounds through, instead of thinking them through. It is better to cry than to worry, better to feel your wounds than to understand them, better to let them enter into your silence than to talk about them. The choice you face constantly is whether you are taking your wounds to your head or your heart.'

I think most of us understand what Nouwen is saying here, even though we resist the advice he gives. We have to feel our pain. Ronald Rolheiser like Nouwen, speaks of the need to experience our emotional life rather than to shut it off. Sadly, there is something in us that does not want to cry, does not want to feel our hurt, does not want to take our pain to a place of silence, and does not want to take our wounds to our heart. I once saw an Argos poster that read, 'Crying is the wise man's violence.'

So instead of feeling our pain, we try to rationalise everything in our heads. Sometimes we pretend things have not happened. We cut people off who have hurt us; anything rather than letting ourselves simply feel our pain. We blame, we do not simply and honestly admit and own our own pain, our own helplessness, our own weakness, and our own inadequacy because it hurts too much. What Henri Nouwen reminds us of, is that we more easily take things to the head than to the heart. That can happen even when we think we are not doing it, which means, of course, that at an emotional level, we never experience freedom and, a bit like acid reflux disease, it keeps coming back. You have to feel it. C.S. Lewis wrote in his book, 'The problem of pain'; 'Mental pain is less dramatic than physical pain, but it is more common and also harder to bear. The frequent attempt to conceal mental pain increases the burden: it is easier to say, 'my tooth is aching' than to say, 'my heart is broken'. Yet if the cause is accepted and faced, the conflict will strengthen and purify the character, and in time the pain will usually pass. Sometimes, however, it persists, and the effect is devastating; if the cause is not faced or not recognised, it produces the dreary state of the chronic neurotic.'

It is frightening how much damage we can do ourselves by holding on to things and not letting go. We hold on to pain and hurt and frustration. We live in fear of people finding out what we are really like, our vulnerability and inadequacy, and so we create our false persona to protect ourselves. Of course, that stops us living in this world filled with wonder, awe and delight. It stops us seeing and knowing that God is present with us. The less you hold on to, the less you protect, then the less frightened you are. Letting go frees you to find life. That is why the spiritual life is never about what you have but always about letting go and somehow, I think, that is the wisdom we are given to teach the world. As nations we must find a way to let go of the pain and hurts of the past. We have to let go of our need for control and we have to be willing to share more equitably the world's resources which means a letting go of something of our own life-styles for the sake of others. It is the only thing that will save the world, but it begins within me. We have to have broken within us the cycle of fear and the need to protect ourselves if we are to show others that wisdom.

One of the truths I am sure of is that I do not have the power to do it. I cannot banish my own fear or the desire to protect myself. It is not possible, but I know that with God everything is possible. That revolution of heart and mind in which we begin the process of letting go is the action of the Spirit, the Spirit who tells us, 'You are loved by God; there is no need to be afraid'. As we become more and more aware of the Spirit at work within us, we become more aware of the invitation Jesus is giving us to trust in the God who has conquered fear. We hear more and more fully the invitation to live in that place where we are constantly willing to let go of what we hold on to so that we can experience life. God can free us so that we learn how to delight and how to look at life without anger or bitterness, but instead be filled with amazement and astonishment at what we see. The pain of letting go is a small price to pay for that experience of living in this world, delighting in everything and free to be yourself and to do what God invites you to do. So, Matthew's Jesus invites us to a true and lasting freedom. He invites us to find the promised land within and to delight in the life that we have to live.

CONCLUSION

When I was a Parish priest, I met two elderly sisters who were the pillars of the parish. They were very elderly and the sort of people who you might think would not be very open to change. However, Peggy and Tess became my friends and I would often call into their house where time seemed to have stood still. That very timelessness would restore my spirit and soothe my mind. They would drink tea with me and, in a very gentle way, would impart the wisdom gained from long lives of prayer and faithfulness. One day I had a particularly bruising encounter with a parishioner and was venting my spleen, when Peggy said to me, 'Well, it is just as well we do not all see things in the same way'.

As I read the Gospels, I realise more and more that Matthew, Mark, Luke and John are presenting four completely different images of Christ, yet with a great degree of unity. They do this because they all see him differently. To be faithful to New Testament theology we have to be faithful to pluralism. We have different Christologies in the New Testament, as communities struggle to understand who Christ is. We have different ecclesiologies in the New Testament. The understanding of Church is always growing and developing, and one writer sees it in a very different way from another.

This book has been an attempt to look at those different reflections about Christ and see how we might respond to them. I hope it has been done in an accessible way. As I have said, the Gospels were never meant to be biographies of Jesus, but a means by which the early church wanted to communicate his presence. So, I often find myself reflecting on what it means to know the presence of God and what my image of God is. The more I can reflect on Christ and what these Gospel writers reveal, the more I can enter into Christ's presence. All of it is a journey and what is more important than anything else is that we remain open on that journey.

Whatever else the Gospels tell us, they do reveal to us a God of love, mercy, compassion and forgiveness whose very desire is to set people free. All my books have only one purpose in mind; that we would know that God more and more fully. If only we could realise how much we are loved, what freedom that would bring. It would bring freedom from undue stress and worry that we think we have no control over. It would grace us to have the freedom to live in the present moment, delighting in it and open to the excitement of it. It would free us from thinking or believing that we have to be anything other than the child we are. It would bring us freedom from ourselves, as we learn to laugh at the foibles that make us who we are. It would give us the freedom to bring to God whatever we had to bring, knowing that it would be met with love. It would remind us that we live in this world with the knowledge that we are living in something far bigger than ourselves. We live in the eternal now, which we are caught up in.

That enables us to have us the freedom to love our brothers and sisters without an agenda. It means that we can accept and include, rather than reject and exclude. It enables us to enter into dialogue with the world from a place of openness rather than suspicion, knowing that everything is gift from the one who is always the lover. That, as Gandhi said, would transform the world.

Open your heart to love and you will find freedom and new life for yourself and the world you live in. Open your heart to love and you will discover the presence of God whose very nature is love. The invitation that I hope this book has brought, is to explore the different understandings of Christ that the Gospels give us. Then we are invited to trust that love, surrender to the Spirit and enter into the freedom it brings.

Further copies of this book
and other books by Fr Chris Thomas

Love is The Key
When Did we Stop Skipping?
Meta... What?
Holiness is for Everyone
Forgiveness is for Giving
Let it Begin With Me
Give Thanks with a Grateful Heart

are available from:

Goodnews Books
Upper Level
St John's Church
296 Sundon Park Road
Luton, Beds, LU3 3AL

01582 571011
www.goodnewsbooks.co.uk
orders@goodnewsbooks.co.uk